**BATTLES**
THAT CHANGED THE WORLD

FIRST BATTLE OF THE MARNE

GETTYSBURG

HASTINGS

MARATHON

MIDWAY

NORMANDY

SARATOGA

TENOCHTITLAN

TET OFFENSIVE

WATERLOO

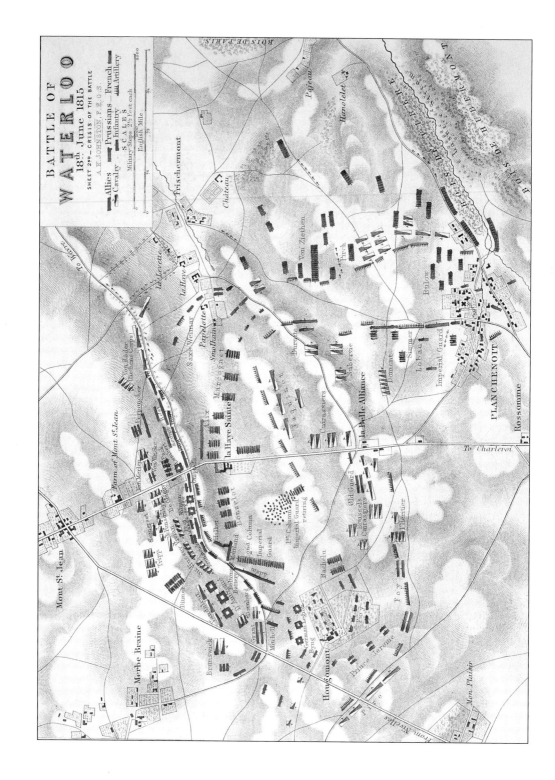

BATTLE OF
WATERLOO
18th June 1815

SHEET 2nd — CRISIS OF THE BATTLE

A.K. JOHNSTON, F.R.G.S.

Allies          Prussians    French
Cavalry        Infantry      Artillery

SCALES
Military Steps 2½ Feet each
English Mile

**BATTLES**
THAT CHANGED THE WORLD

# WATERLOO

## SAMUEL WILLARD CROMPTON

**CHELSEA HOUSE PUBLISHERS**
PHILADELPHIA

*Frontispiece:* The map shows the dispositions in the morning hours. The British, in red, are drawn up on the slopes that lead to Mont St. Jean, and the French are deployed on a wide front, with their center at La Belle Alliance. The British defenses were formidable, and Marshal Soult recommended a maneuver around them, but Napoleon refused.

**CHELSEA HOUSE PUBLISHERS**

EDITOR IN CHIEF  Sally Cheney
DIRECTOR OF PRODUCTION  Kim Shinners
CREATIVE MANAGER  Takeshi Takahashi
MANUFACTURING MANAGER  Diann Grasse

**STAFF FOR WATERLOO**

EDITOR  Lee Marcott
PICTURE RESEARCHER  Pat Burns
PRODUCTION ASSISTANT  Jaimie Winkler
SERIES AND COVER DESIGNER  Keith Trego
LAYOUT  21st Century Publishing and Communications, Inc.

http://www.chelseahouse.com

First Printing

1 3 5 7 9 8 6 4 2

**Library of Congress Cataloging-in-Publication Data**

Crompton, Samuel Willard.
  Waterloo / Samuel Crompton.
    p. cm. — (Battles that changed the world)
Includes bibliographical references and index.
  ISBN 0-7910-6683-5 — ISBN 0-7910-7110-3 (pbk.)
  1. Waterloo (Belgium), Battle of, 1815—Juvenile literature. 2. Napoleon I, Emperor of the French, 1769–1821—Military leadership—Juvenile literature. 3. Wellington, Arthur Wellesley, Duke of, 1769–1852—Military leadership—Juvenile literature. 4. Napoleonic Wars, 1800–1815—Campaigns—Belgium—Waterloo—Juvenile literature. 5. Armies—Europe—History—19th century—Juvenile literature. I. Title. II. Series.
DC242 .C955 2002
940.2'7—dc21

2002000605

# TABLE OF CONTENTS

# The Corsican Returns

Napoleon bade farewell to his Imperial Guard at Fontainebleau in April 1814. The Emperor and his hardy followers were commemorated in this painting by Horace Vernet, done between 1814 and 1825.

*"Soldiers! I heard your call while I was in exile. I have come, despite every obstacle and every peril."*

Napoleon Bonaparte

The first of March in 1815 was like any other day on France's Mediterranean coast. Gentle waves caressed the empty beaches around the towns of Nice, Cannes, and Monaco. Clouds drifted overhead, indicating late winter snows in the mountains. Some time early that afternoon, a large group of men disembarked from a series of long boats, and occupied the beach known as Golfe Juan. Their leader was Napoleon Bonaparte, and they were about to commence the action known ever since as the "Hundred Days."

On the beach, Napoleon issued a manifesto, addressed to the veterans of his many campaigns.

Soldiers!

We have not been defeated. Two men left our ranks and betrayed their fellows, their Prince, their benefactor . . . .

Soldiers! I heard your call while I was in exile; I have come despite every obstacle and every peril.

Your general, called to the throne by the choice of the people, and elevated by you, has returned, come and join him.

Bring back the colors that the nation has proscribed, and which, for 25 years, served to terrify the enemies of France. Bring back the tricolor, that you carried in those great days!

You have been asked to forget that you are the Master of Nations, but we cannot forgive those who meddle in our affairs. Who pretends to be your master? Who has such power? Take back the Eagles you carried at Ulm, at Austerlitz, at Iena, at Eylau, at Friedland, at Tudella, at Eckmuhl, at Essling, at Wagram, at Smolensk, at Moskow, at Lutzen, at Wurchen, at Montmiral.

Signed, Napoleon.

Having made this dramatic proclamation, Napoleon marched north from Golfe Juan, located very close to the town of Cannes on the French Riviera.

It was a daring gamble, even for this man who was known for his belief in Destiny, and his willingness to risk a roll of the dice.

Born in Corsica in 1769, Napoleon had left home to

In late February 1815, Napoleon took the biggest risk of his career. He and several hundred loyal followers embarked from Elba, headed for the south coast of France.

attend military school in France at the age of nine. He had risen slowly in the ranks until the French Revolution of 1789, which had afforded him opportunities to display his genius for war. He had risen to general by 1796, first consul in 1800, and emperor of France in 1804. It was a stunning rise for someone who was not French, but from the island of Corsica which had been conquered by France in 1768, one year before his birth.

In March 1815, Napoleon had been in exile for the past 10 months. Defeated by the allied governments of Britain, Prussia, Austria, and Russia, he had abdicated his throne in April 1814. Loud had been the cries of "Hang Bonaparte," but Czar Alexander of Russia had persuaded the other allied leaders to allow Napoleon a comfortable exile on the island of Elba, located between the west coast of Italy and the east coast of Corsica. There the former Emperor could rule, with about 1,000 of his trusted Imperial Guardsmen.

Napoleon had gone to Elba in April 1814; in that same month, King Louis XVIII had returned to Paris to rule as the restored Bourbon monarch. The king returned a stranger to the Parisians, and indeed to the nation as a whole. He was the younger brother of King Louis XVI who had gone to the guillotine in 1793 (Louis XVI and Marie Antoinette's son had died in prison, creating the space between Louis XVI and Louis XVIII).

Having spent most of his life as a political exile in England, King Louis XVIII wanted to create as fresh a start as possible. He disregarded the advice of his younger brother, who wanted to return everything to the way it had been prior to the French Revolution of 1789. Louis XVIII granted a Charter (constitution) to the French people. He governed with a two-house legislature, modeled on the British Parliament, although the right to vote was severely restricted, limited to men of wealth and property. Most important, Louis XVIII abolished the conscription that had been so important to the armies of the French Revolution and Napoleon. This move was the most popular of Louis XVIII's reign.

Meanwhile, the diplomats and leaders of the allied nations met at the Congress of Vienna. They settled on peace terms that were quite lenient. France had to withdraw to its boundaries of 1792—that was all. There was no indemnity and no punishment for the 20 years of warfare that had begun in 1793. The reasons for the lenity were twofold. First, Czar Alexander of Russia insisted that it would be unfair to blame a nation for the actions of one man; second, the French foreign minister, Talleyrand, artfully conspired to divide the Allies amongst themselves. He had succeeded by the start of 1815, and there was every reason to expect that Europe would settle into a long period of peaceful recovery.

Then Napoleon landed at Golfe Juan.

He had only about 1,000 men. King Louis XVIII had a regular army of about 120,000. If ever a revolt or an uprising should have been suppressed, this was the one. But such numerical calculations do not take into account the brilliant gamble Napoleon played, or his consummate skill in winning men over to his cause.

The news reached Paris on March 5. The king hardly believed what he was told, but he summoned his military leaders, among whom there were several of Napoleon's former marshals. Marshals MacDonald and Soult reaffirmed their allegiance to the new Bourbon government. Marshal Michel Ney went so far as to vow he would bring the former emperor back to Paris in an iron cage.

Two days later, on March 7, the news reached Vienna, where the Congress was in session. Klemmens von Metternich, the Austrian prime minister, swiftly obtained pledges of fealty from each one of the allied governments; they would not rest until the usurper Napoleon was defeated. Even Napoleon's wife, the Empress Marie-Louise, issued a statement that she had no wish to return to her husband or to France. Her son, Napoleon's only child, was taken away from his French nurse, and kept a virtual prisoner at the palace of Schonnbrunn.

Everyone waited to see what would happen. Would Napoleon fight a battle against the best of his former marshals?

One of the most dramatic events in French history took place on the afternoon of March 7. On the same day that the allied powers swore to defeat Napoleon, the adventurer and his group met a column of French army troops, of the Fifth Regiment, in a mountain pass north of Grasse, in southern France. Napoleon had known this moment would come, and he was ready. As the two groups approached one another, Napoleon ordered his men to keep their guns at their sides and wait, while he walked forward, alone. As he came within range of the men sent to arrest him, Napoleon called out:

"Soldiers of the Fifth, do you recognize me?"

They did. Ignoring the orders of their officers, the soldiers threw their guns aside and shouted "Vive L'Empereur!" In one stunning encounter, Napoleon had defeated the hopes of those who supported the Bourbon cause.

From there he went from strength to strength. He entered Lyons, the second largest French city, on March 10. Three days later, he sent a short message to Marshal Ney, encouraging him to desert the Bourbon ranks and bring his men over to Napoleon. Remarkably this

Soldiers were sent to arrest Napoleon. He met them with "Here is your Emperor, shoot if you will!" They flocked to him and his contingent.

too occurred. The Napoleonic magic was too strong to resist.

King Louis XVIII learned of Ney's defection on March 17. His only comment was "Is there no more honor?" The aged, infirm monarch knew he was about

## Napoleon's Family

Carlo and Letizia Bonaparte were members of the Corsican nobility. They had eight children, the second oldest of whom was Napoleon. Once he became emperor of the French in 1804, Napoleon began to award titles and lands to his siblings.

The eldest in the family, Joseph, became king of Naples, then king of Spain. Louis Bonaparte, nine years younger than Napoleon, was made king of Holland. The youngest of the brothers, Jerome, became king of Westphalia, which was carved out of Prussia, in 1807.

Nor did Napoleon neglect his sisters. Pauline, who was 11 years younger than Napoleon, became duchess of Guastalla in northern Italy. Caroline, who was the sibling most akin to Napoleon in terms of ambition, became queen of Naples in 1808. Eliza became grand duchess of Tuscany in 1809.

One of the most astute comments concerning queen Caroline of Naples came from the French diplomat Talleyrand. Looking at the nude done of Caroline by the artist Canova, Talleyrand remarked, "The head of Cromwell on a pretty woman!" A dangerous combination indeed.

By about 1810, virtually all members of the family had been provided for. Father Carlo had passed on, but mother Letizia was still the leader of the family. When Napoleon boasted and strutted his performances on the world stage, she usually responded, "If it lasts! If it all lasts!"

As we know, the Napoleonic dynasties did not last. Napoleon's Russian campaign in 1812, and his defeat at Leipzig in 1813 signaled the end of his fortunes. By the time he abdicated in 1814, virtually all his brothers and sisters had lost their crowns and titles as well.

But it was not the end of the Bonapartes, not by a long shot. In 1848, Louis-Napoleon, son of the man who had been king of Holland, won election as the new French president. His name recognition was enough to win him 5.5 million votes out of a total of 8 million cast. Louis-Napoleon was president of the French Republic from 1849 until 1851, when he carried out a military coup. In 1852, he became

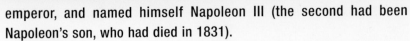

emperor, and named himself Napoleon III (the second had been Napoleon's son, who had died in 1831).

Napoleon III ruled France from 1852 until 1870, when France lost the Franco-Prussian War. He went into retirement in England and died soon after.

Little known, today, is the Bonaparte branch that came to America. Jerome Bonaparte, the king of Westphalia, had married an American woman and had a child before Napoleon forced the younger brother to have a divorce. Jerome Bonaparte II grew up in Baltimore. His son, Charles Joseph Bonaparte, was born there in 1851. Charles became a lawyer and a civil servant whose major interest was in civil service reform. He became good friends with Theodore Roosevelt and when Roosevelt entered the White House in 1901, he made Bonaparte first one of the Board of Indian Commissioners, then secretary of the U.S. Navy, and finally U.S. attorney general in 1906. One of his most enduring legacies was the creation of the new Bureau of Investigation which later evolved into the F.B.I.

to commence once more on the travels and exile that had been the dominant feature of his adult life. On the morning of March 19, the king and his entourage fled Paris for the Belgian border; one day later Napoleon entered Paris in triumph.

Napoleon had escaped Elba and reached Paris with hardly firing a shot. The Bourbon rule had collapsed as the emperor moved north and reclaimed his domains. There was at least some truth to the Napoleonic claim that the nation welcomed him. It may not have invited him, but it accepted his reappearance.

The Duke of Wellington, painted around 1815. The pose, posture, and facial expression are all meant to convey that this man was cool, calculating, and in control. This painting of Britain's foremost hero is in the Victoria and Albert Museum in London.

# Wellington's Invincibles

*"It is for you to save the world again."*

Czar Alexander of Russia

The average British subject was enjoying a well-earned period of rest in the early spring of 1815. Then he or she opened the newspaper on Saturday, March 11.

Early yesterday morning we received by express from Dover, the important but lamentable intelligence of a civil war having been again kindled in France, by that wretch Buonoparte (*sic*), whose life was so impoliticly spared by the allied sovereigns. It now appears that the hypocritical villain, who, at the time of his cowardly abdication, affected an aversion to the shedding of blood in a civil warfare, has been employed during the whole time of his residence at Elba, in carrying on secret and treasonable intrigues with the tools of his former crimes in France.

*The London Times*, March 11, 1815

At such a time, the British public and the British government were accustomed to relying on the cool and calm manner of the Duke of Wellington. Britain's greatest soldier, however, was not in the home land. He was in Vienna, serving as the emissary to the Congress.

On March 7, 1815, members of the Congress of Vienna learned of Napoleon's escape from Elba. Consternation prevailed among the delegates. One of the crowned heads of state, Czar Alexander of Russia, placed his hand on the shoulder of the Duke of Wellington, and said, "It is for you to save the world again."

Arthur Wellesley was born in Dublin, Ireland, on May 1, 1769. He was just three and a half months older than Napoleon Bonaparte, but the two were born into very different circumstances. Wellesley belonged to the Anglo-Irish aristocracy which owned most of the Irish land, and represented that country in the British Parliament.

Wellesley joined the British army in 1787. He began as an ensign, and was promoted to lieutenant that same year. He took time out from the army to serve as a member of Parliament for Trim, Ireland, in 1790, but returned to military service within one year.

The British army that Wellington entered was not in one of its finer moments. The British had suffered some humiliating losses during the American War for Independence (American Revolution), and the British leadership still employed the same type of thinking that had prevailed for about a century. Until he sailed for India in June 1796, Arthur Wellesley seemed likely to be one of those leaders who continued the old fashions, rather than shape new ones.

In 1796, India was partially under British control, but it was not officially part of the British Empire. The British possessions in India were governed and managed by the East India Company rather than the crown. Like many officers before and after, Wellesley had to cooperate with merchants and officials of the East India Company in order to fulfill his military duties. The situation did not change until 1859, when India officially entered the British Empire.

As lieutenant colonel of the Thirty-Third Regiment, Wellesley entered a new and unfamiliar world in India. The British sections of that land were menaced by native revolts, some of which were engineered by French sympathizers. France and Britain had been at war since France had beheaded King Louis XVI in 1793, and part of Wellesley's efforts in India would be part of the worldwide war between those nations.

During eight years in India, Wellesley became a seasoned commander. He led combinations of British and native troops, and won the majority of his battles. When historians are pressed to elaborate on the reason for Wellesley's success, they usually turn to two things: supplies and terrain. Wellesley was active in managing the delivery of supplies; therefore his men believed that he cared for them. He was even more involved in selecting the ground on which they would fight, and therefore he began most battles with the advantage of knowing the terrain better than did his opponents.

Wellesley returned to England in 1805, just weeks before Admiral Nelson won the naval Battle of Trafalgar. This battle ensured that Napoleon would not be able to invade England, but how could the British strike against 'Boney,' considering that his was the largest and best army in Europe? The answer came in 1807, when Napoleon invaded Spain and placed his brother Joseph on its throne.

The British government decided this was the time to mount an expeditionary force against the French. When British troops landed in Portugal in 1808, Wellesley was second in command to Sir John Moore, a brilliant and dedicated soldier. The British won some initial victories, but then were chased to the port of Corunna, where Sir John Moore died in the fighting. The British were evacuated by sea, and with Moore gone, Wellesley was the natural choice for the new commander.

Wellesley landed in Portugal in 1809 as the commander in chief. He made an alliance with the Portuguese who detested Napoleon, and he prepared to move into Spain when it was possible. Prior to that, however, Wellesley fortified a series of mountains across the whole of southern Portugal, which gave him a virtually impregnable fortress from which to work. Secure in this, he was able to go to battle knowing he had an excellent place to which he could retreat.

Far away in Paris, Emperor Napoleon did not take the threat of the British or of Arthur Wellesley very seriously. He sent one marshal after another over the Pyrenee Mountains into Spain, telling each one to clean up the British and Portuguese. It took some time, but each marshal returned in succession, with his head hung low. The lack of supplies, the poor road system, and the use of 'guerrilla' (the word entered the English language as a result of this very war) warfare by the Spanish ground the French forces down. When they did meet Arthur Wellesley in battle, he nearly always defeated them through his selection of the terrain, and his keen direction of the battle's progress. By early 1812, the situation had become critical for the French; they were being pushed back toward France itself.

Meanwhile, many British soldiers and officers had made names for themselves. One was Peregrine Maitland. Born in Hampshire County, England, in 1777, Maitland joined the British Grenadier Guards in 1792, just one year prior to the outbreak of the Revolutionary Wars. He rose rapidly from ensign to lieutenant colonel in 1803. He landed with the first British forces in Spain and earned a medal for his performance at Corunna in 1809. Maitland was second in command in the British attack on Seville, and commanded the first brigade of Grenadier Guards at the Battle of Nivelle, in the operations before Bayonne. He became a major-general in 1814.

The climactic battle of the Peninsular (Spanish) War was fought at Vittoria on June 21, 1813. Wellington smashed the French army and captured most of their baggage and equipment. King Joseph of Spain, Napoleon's older brother, fled across the Pyrenees into France, and the long, grueling Spanish campaign was finally over.

Wellesley was rewarded. King George III made him the Duke of Wellington, and he was acclaimed as Britain's greatest soldier, and the great rival to Napoleon Bonaparte. The two men had not yet met on the field, but public perception was that they were the greatest military leaders of the day.

Early in 1814, Wellington crossed the Pyrenees and invaded southern France. At the same time, Austrian,

Fought in 1813, the Battle of Vittoria was the culmination of all that the Duke of Wellington had tried to achieve in Spain. His victory that day raised him to a level where only one living soldier could be compared to him: Napoleon.

Prussian, and Russian armies invaded France from the east. Faced by this massive coalition of foes, Napoleon Bonaparte abdicated his throne in April, and was exiled to the island of Elba.

Wellington's services remained very much in demand. In the autumn of 1814, the British government asked him if he was willing to go to North America, to serve as commander in chief against the Americans, who had declared war on Great Britain in June 1812. This war, known in America as the War of 1812, had been a sideshow for the British till now, but with Napoleon defeated, they wanted to see the Americans humbled. The British ministry promised Wellington all the support in men and material he might need.

To the great surprise of the government, Wellington turned the request down. He was too good a soldier to say "no" to his government, but in a long letter he made it plain that he believed the war against the Americans was unwinnable. As long as Britain lacked naval superiority on the Great Lakes (Lake Ontario in particular), Wellington believed any future campaigns there would be ineffective.

Impressed by the assessment of their best soldier, the British leaders decided to come to terms with their former colonists. The peace treaty of Ghent was signed on December 24, 1814, bringing the War of 1812 to an end.

News traveled slowly in those days. The British ship that carried the good news of the peace treaty did not reach New York City until about February 10, and Washington D.C. until two days later. Meanwhile, the last battle of the war had been fought. General Andrew Jackson had led the American defense of New Orleans. The British, led by General Pakenham who was brother-in-law to the Duke of Wellington, attacked the American defenses on the morning of January 8, 1815. Safe behind their earthworks, the American riflemen devastated the British, causing nearly 2,000 casualties.

On January 8, 1815, British soldiers attacked entrenched Americans outside of New Orleans. The carnage was fearful; nearly 2,000 British soldiers were killed, wounded, or missing. Sir Edward Pakenham, the British leader, was killed early in the fighting. He was the brother-in-law of the Duke of Wellington.

The British then withdrew, leaving the field and the city to the Americans.

It is a tragedy that so many men lost their lives needlessly in the Battle of New Orleans. The great losses suffered that day, and the fact they might have

# King George III

Americans remember him primarily as the "king who lost the colonies," but many Britons recall him as the king who presided over the start of the Industrial Revolution, and whose reign witnessed the defeat of the Corsican tyrant Napoleon. He was long lived, and it is sometimes difficult to remember that this king took the throne in 1760 when there were still 13 American colonies, and passed away in 1820 when there were 18 American states.

Born in 1738, George was 22 when he succeeded to the throne in 1760. For the next 20 years he made what are considered to have been poor choices in his prime ministers, and by 1783 he had to acknowledge the former American colonies as "free and independent States." His reign, however, was not even half over.

During the decade of the 1790s, King George alternated between the leadership and the policies of Charles James Fox and William Pitt the Younger. The nation was well governed during these years, and Britons enjoyed a new camaraderie as they faced their old enemy, France.

Napoleon won the Battle of Austerlitz in 1805, and William Pitt the Younger died the next year. Not only did the British leadership exhibit serious weakness over the next five years, but King George himself fell into what has been called the "Royal Malady." He was pronounced insane in 1811.

While King George was under the care of numerous doctors, his oldest son, George, took the leadership as prince regent. The son's flagrant spending and dissolute habits worked to ensure the continuing popularity of his mentally ill father. The British people began to forget some of the mistakes George III had made, and chose to remember his sterling character, faithfulness to duty, and sober habits. Then came the second war with the Americans.

In June 1812, the United States declared war on Great Britain over matters which revolved around British impressment of American

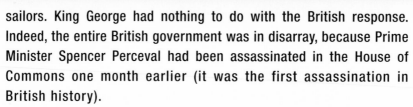

sailors. King George had nothing to do with the British response. Indeed, the entire British government was in disarray, because Prime Minister Spencer Perceval had been assassinated in the House of Commons one month earlier (it was the first assassination in British history).

The war against the United States was very popular in Britain, because the British believed the Americans had "stabbed them in the back" while they were fighting Napoleon. Consequently, King George III's popularity increased during the war, while his son fell more and more into disrepute.

The war against the Americans ended officially on Christmas Eve 1814, and the Hundred Days campaign of Napoleon ended in July 1815. Britons settled down to a well-deserved period of rest.

King George III died in 1820, and was succeeded by his son, who became King George IV. Both George IV and William IV who succeeded him were seen as failures in the monarchy, and only when Victoria took the throne in 1838 did the British people start to believe once more that they had a monarch in whom they could believe.

been prevented, is one reason why historians sometimes call the War of 1812, the "War of Faulty Communication."

News of the disaster at New Orleans reached London about the first of March, 1815. The British were indignant and upset, but one week later they read the much more distressing news that Napoleon Bonaparte had escaped from Elba and was about to threaten the peace of Europe for a second time. As Czar Alexander said to the Duke of Wellington, "It is for you to save the world again." We have no record of Wellington's reply, but we can imagine that he might have thought it was not only up to him, but also up to the men who had soldiered so well under him in Spain, and who would have gone to America. They were the veterans of the campaigns in Portugal and Spain, and they called themselves "Wellington's Invincibles."

# Prussian Hussar

The turning point in Napoleon's career was his retreat from Moscow. Were it not for the heroics of Marshal Ney, even fewer of the French would have survived the disastrous retreat. Napoleon's failure to defeat Russia caused other nations, Prussia in particular, to rise up against him.

*"It is the greatest piece of good luck."*

Field Marshal Blücher

During the night of March 8, 1815, a 72-year-old man was wakened from his sleep by an aide who told him Napoleon had escaped from Elba. One might expect the old soldier to be dismayed, but Field Marshal Blücher replied:

"It is the greatest piece of good luck that could have happened to Prussia! Now the war will begin again! The armies will fight and make good all the faults committed in Vienna!"

Difficult news had never swayed Blücher. Those who knew him best declared he had never turned back from a fight in his life.

Gebhard Lebrecht Blücher was born in Rostock, Prussia, on December 16, 1742, making him 26 years older than both Napoleon and Wellington. Blücher was the eighth of nine sons in the family; all the sons joined armies when the Seven Years' War broke out in 1756, but not the same ones.

Although they were a Prussian family, the Blücher sons lent their services to several different armies and kings. Gebhard joined the army of the king of Sweden in 1757, and wound up fighting against the Prussian army led by King Frederick II (later known as "Frederick the Great").

In 1759, Blücher was captured by a unit of Prussian horsemen known as the Black Hussars. The Hussar commander recognized Blücher, and asked him to change sides, to fight with the army of his fatherland. Blücher agreed, and by 1760 he was a captain of the Hussars, with an excellent fighting record.

Prussia was fighting for her life against France, Austria, Russia, and Sweden, but she had a genius in her leader. King Frederick held out just long enough, so that he was saved by a surprise. Czarina Elizabeth died in 1762. Czar Peter II, her successor, was a great admirer of Frederick the Great. The Russians pulled out of the war, and the other enemies folded up from exhaustion. In the peace treaty of 1763, Prussia remained an important force on the map of Europe.

Blücher remained in the Hussars until 1773. Upset because a junior officer was promoted over him, Blücher resigned that year and married the daughter of a prominent farmer. Within two years' time, the rambunctious cavalryman had become an excellent family man and a fairly good gentleman farmer. He did not return to military service until 1787 after the death of Frederick the Great.

Prussia's great king had been deeply irritated by Blücher's resignation, and he refused all requests from the aging soldier to be reinstated. But Frederick died in 1786 and his son took Blücher back as a major in the Black

Hussars. He was now about 45 and much older than most cavalrymen, but Blücher never let age slow him down. He became a demanding but popular leader in the regiment.

Prussia went to war with Revolutionary France in 1792. Both Prussia and Austria hoped to squelch the Revolution and put King Louis XVI back on the throne. Instead, the king was guillotined in 1793, and both Prussia and Austria were hard pressed to defend themselves from the fury of the Revolutionary armies.

We tend to think of the armies of Napoleon and the Revolution as "professional" ones, but the real genius of the Revolutionary forces was their spirit. The French recruits flowed around their more static foes, outmaneuvered them, and were better at getting food from the countryside (we could say they were better at stealing from the peasants!). For all these reasons, the French defeated many of their enemies, and truly professional soldiers such as Blücher were astonished by their success.

Prussia withdrew from the war in 1795. Blücher remained in uniform and he rose to the rank of general by 1800. Again, he was much older than his peers, but his early service under Frederick the Great and his keen eye for a battlefield made him one of the most valued officers in Prussia. It was, after all, a country with a great military tradition. The French philosopher Voltaire had once described Prussia as an "army that has a country," rather than the other way around.

That tradition and pride were deeply wounded when Prussia declared war on Napoleon Bonaparte in 1806. Napoleon had provoked the declaration, using excuses to seize sections of Prussian land, and Prussia was in for the worst licking of her life. In the summer of 1806, Napoleon defeated two separate Prussian armies at the Battles of Iena and Auerstadt. Blücher was among the defeated and he surrendered to become a French prisoner.

A portrait of then-General Blücher painted in about 1802. His moustache, sword, and Iron Cross all indicate Blücher is part of the famed Prussian Army. This painting was made before the disastrous campaign of 1806, in which Napoleon defeated the Prussians and imposed harsh terms of peace upon them.

In 1807, the Prussian prisoner met Napoleon Bonaparte for the first time. Blücher was brought to Napoleon's headquarters at Kirkenstein castle. The Frenchman thrust out his hand and announced he was pleased to meet the "bravest Prussian general." Blücher responded with warmth, and the two men sized one another up.

Despite his strength and vigor, Napoleon was a small man. Blücher towered over the Frenchman, who was 26 years younger. The two may have recognized something similar in each other. Both men were relentless fighters, always optimistic, even when the odds were against them. Had Napoleon been able to win Blücher to the French cause, military history might have taken a very different course.

But Blücher went home in a prisoner exchange that same year, and King Frederick William of Prussia signed an alliance with Napoleon in 1812. To the shame of Blücher and other patriotic Prussians, the treaty required Prussia to contribute men to Napoleon's planned invasion of Russia. The only consolation Blücher had that year was his promotion to lieutenant general.

In June 1812, Napoleon invaded Russia. His 600,000-man army was composed of Frenchmen, Austrians, Prussians, and others. The "Grand Armee" moved across great swathes of territory and reached Moscow in September. Napoleon hoped that Czar Alexander would then sue for peace, but the Czar was adamant; he would not negotiate while there was one Frenchman left on Russian soil. Making matters worse, there was a severe fire in Moscow. Many buildings were destroyed, and Napoleon was thereby deprived of safe winter quarters. He turned his army for home.

The long retreat across the Russian and Polish plains was a catastrophe for Napoleon and his men. Only about 50,000 of the 600,000 men who had left home in the spring of 1812 ever returned.

Napoleon quickly raised another army, and fought on. By now, though, his enemies and even his former enemies had taken heart from what had happened in Russia. King Frederick William broke the terms of his alliance, and declared war on Napoleon. So did the Austrian emperor.

Suddenly Napoleon was on the defensive against all of Central and Eastern Europe.

General Blücher played a key role in the many battles of 1813. He led the Prussians at the Battle of Leignitz in April, and again at the Battle of the Nations in October. The second battle, fought near a town called Leipzig, was the decisive one of the campaign. The combination of Russians, Austrians, and Prussians overwhelmed Napoleon and broke his power in Central Europe.

Blücher led the Prussians in their last campaign, the invasion of France in 1814. By now Blücher was seen as the preeminent general on the allied side; his advice was sought by his king and by Czar Alexander as the allied armies entered France, and approached Paris.

Napoleon abdicated his throne in April, a few days after Blücher and the Prussians entered Paris. As he went off into exile, Napoleon remembered that Blücher had been one of his most implacable enemies. The Prussian and Frenchman had met only once in person but they had clashed on the battle-field nearly a dozen times. Now Blücher, along with the other Allies, celebrated while Napoleon was sent to Elba.

When the war finally ended, Blücher was showered with honors. King Frederick William made him a Prussian field marshal. This was the highest achievement any Prussian soldier could attain; it placed Blücher among the great leaders who had served King Frederick the Great during his glory years. The king went even further and made Blücher a Prussian prince. This did not make him one of the royal line, but was a dignity far above that reached by most soldiers.

Surprisingly, the 11 months between Napoleon's abdication and his escape from Elba were not comforting ones for Blücher. As he learned the news of the Congress of Vienna, particularly its territorial decisions, he declared that France had escaped too lightly. She should be made to pay more for

General Blücher shown in about the year 1810. Blücher appears in civilian garb that makes him look more like a Prussian philosopher than a Prussian general. At this time, Napoleon dominated Europe, and Prussia's King William willingly accommodated the Corsican's demands.

her depredations (it was true that France had not even been required to return the art treasures her soldiers had stolen from other European nations). Therefore, he was pleased to hear Napoleon had escaped and the wars had begun once more. It was, he said, "The greatest piece of good luck."

This painting by Horace Vernet shows Napoleon, Marshal Murat, and Marshal Berthier on horseback in 1806. Murat, in a red cavalryman's outfit, was the most dashing and daring of the marshals, and one of the best cavalrymen of any time period. Berthier was the coordinator of Napoleon's plans, and his death in June 1815 was a serious loss to Napoleon in the Waterloo campaign.

# Napoleon Strikes!

*"Napoleon has humbugged me, by God!"*

Duke of Wellington

Napoleon made short work of King Louis XVIII and the restored Bourbon administration. Landing in southern France on March first, Napoleon made his way north and on March 20 he entered Paris in triumph. The emperor had returned.

Napoleon professed to want peace, but the allied powers would have none of it. On March 28, Britain, Prussia, Austria, and Russia signed the Treaty of Chaumont, in which they swore to rose an allied army of 600,000 men and crush

Napoleon before he had time to rebuild his strength at home.

Three different armies participated in the campaign that ended at Waterloo. Napoleon led a French army that was relatively homogeneous. It was composed of many veterans of his earlier campaigns with a sprinkling of new blood. Wellington commanded an army very different from what he had led in Spain. There he had led a homogeneous British army; now he had a mixed army of British, Dutch and Belgian troops to lead. For the sake of convenience, they are collectively called the Anglo-Dutch army. Blücher, like Napoleon, commanded a homogeneous army, but he encountered great difficulties in obtaining money supplies because Prussia was drained from years of warfare. Together these three armies—French, Anglo-Dutch, and Prussian— would contest the fields of Quatre-Bras, Ligny, Wavre, and Waterloo.

Each of the three armies was made up of the same rough deployment that had prevailed on European battlefields since the time of the duke of Marlborough, 100 years before. Horse, foot, and guns were the simple way of expressing this disposition; the more sophisticated words are cavalry, infantry, and artillery.

The foot soldier comprised the heart of any army. His willingness to stand and receive fire, or advance with the bayonet, usually determined the outcome of any battle. The British, French, and Prussian soldiers of the day fought with the same types of muskets they had 50 years earlier; the "Brown Bess" musket of the British army had first been issued in 1745.

The artillerymen played a secondary but vital role. Only 30 years earlier, cannon had been too heavy and unwieldy to use effectively on the battlefield. But Napoleon, who had trained as an artilleryman, had pioneered the use of mobile, horse-drawn cannon that could be deployed to great effect. Better than any other commander of the day, Napoleon understood the vital importance of cannon. Consequently, the French army in Belgium deployed more guns than either of its foes.

Cavalry would seem to be doomed as a battlefield formation, but the Napoleonic Wars had actually seen a resurgence of the use of mounted men. Napoleon had added Polish lancers to his cavalry, and the lance had made a comeback since about 1800. Just the same, every top commander knew that infantry deployed in hollow squares could repel almost any cavalry assault. A wise commander kept his cavalry for a key moment when, seeing signs of an enemy weakening, the horses could break a line, and allow for a decisive action.

All three commanders had their areas of specialty. Although he understood a battle and its sequences better than anyone, Napoleon probably placed more reliance on his artillery than the other two segments. Wellington, who understood a battlefield (the terrain) better than anyone else, placed his reliance on the "thin red line" of British infantry. Blücher, who inspired his men to greater heights than any other leader of the day, had been a hussar since 1760, and the cavalry was naturally his favorite wing in the army.

Three armies, three sections of each army, and three brilliant leaders clashed on the Belgian fields in the late spring of 1815.

Everyone expected that Napoleon would have to fight defensively on this occasion. The forces that gathered against him were large, even overwhelming. Between them, Britain, Prussia, Austria, and Russia pledged to raise 500,000 men to bring down the Corsican. No one accepted Napoleon's earnest protestation that this time he meant to rule in peace; the Allies were determined to bring him down.

France had fought great odds before. In 1793, Revolutionary France had declared the *levee en masse*, which meant that each and every member of French society had to contribute something to the military effort. But that was 22 years ago, and France was weary of sacrifices. The best Napoleon could manage was to put together about 120,000 men, meaning that he would eventually face odds of about four-to-one.

Numbers never tell the whole story however. Napoleon was able to recruit these men in about one month, while the Allies, especially far-off Russia, would require months to bring up their full strength. Even more important, Napoleon was able to quickly consolidate the hard core of his army from battle-hardened veterans. Best of all, he was able to persuade nearly all of his former Imperial Guardsmen to the fight. By early June, Napoleon had the makings of one of the most cohesive armies he had ever commanded.

The marshals were another story. Some, like Marmont, stayed in the service of King Louis XVIII. Others, such as Ney, were allowed to serve, but were under a cloud because of their former loyalty to the king. Still others, such as Massena, professed their renewed loyalty to Napoleon, but begged off from active service, alleging physical infirmities.

On April 17, Napoleon awarded the baton of a marshal of France to Emmanuel, Marquis de Grouchy. He was the 26th man to be so honored, and he would be the last. Grouchy had served with the Revolutionary and Napoleonic armies for nearly 20 years, and he had been an excellent cavalry leader in the Russian campaign. But he was unpopular with his fellow marshals, many of whom questioned the need for another to join their ranks.

A conscription scene typical of the years 1813-1814 when men were enrolled into the military service for the Napoleonic Wars.

The greatest loss by far was that of Marshal Berthier, Napoleon's longtime chief of staff. Berthier, whose career had begun in 1780, serving with the French army during the War of the American Revolution, was a peerless coordinator. He was able to interpret Napoleon's orders and distribute them with precision and speed. Berthier's demise was reported in *The London Times* of Saturday, June 17, 1815:

> Respecting the death of Prince Berthier, private letters from Bamberg communicate the following: "At the moment when a Russian division was passing through Bamberg, the Prince came to a window in the attics of the palace, and found there a lady in the suite of Princess Wilhelmma of Bavaria. He asked her whether she did not wish to have a nearer view of the fine troops that were passing. The lady had scarcely left the room, and proceeded to a gallery with this view, when the Prince shut the door, threw himself out of the window, and was killed on the spot."

Time was clearly against Napoleon. Given enough weeks and months, the Austrians and Russians would mobilize vast numbers of men who would grind him down to the dust. But if he could score a lightning-fast victory, reminiscent of his former glory, perhaps Austria and Russia could be persuaded to make peace. Therefore, Napoleon decided to strike fast and strike first, against the British and Prussians.

The Duke of Wellington did not return to England once he learned of Napoleon's return; there was no time for a visit home. Instead, Wellington made his way across Western Europe and reached Belgium, where he, like Napoleon, began to consolidate an army.

Unlike Napoleon, Wellington was unable to put together the best of his former armies. Some regiments were still in North America; others had been sent to India; and still others had to recruit to reach their full strength. So, although he had staff and supply masters from the Spanish campaigns, Wellington had to fight without most of the men who had been his "Invincibles" between 1808 and 1814. Wellington put together a mixed army: there were British, Dutch, Belgian, and even a few German soldiers. Remarkably, he was able to weld them together in the few weeks that remained to him. Wellington had no illusions about them men he commanded. On May 8th, he wrote a letter to Lord Stewart, who had been his adjutant general in Spain:

> I have got a very infamous army, very weak and ill equipped, and a very inexperienced staff. In my opinion they are doing nothing in England. They have not raised a man; they have not called out the militia either in England or Ireland; are unable to send me any thing; and they have not sent a message to Parliament about the money. The war spirit is therefore evaporating as I am informed.

Blücher, in Prussia, had a different set of problems. Prussia was a country that depended on its army at all times, and as such, forces were seldom disbanded. Within two weeks of learning of Napoleon's return, Blücher had put together one of the best Prussian armies to date, numbering about 107,000 men.

Common sense seemed to indicate that Napoleon should fight a defensive campaign, centered on a ring of forts around Paris. He had fought just such a campaign in the early spring of 1814, and had inflicted

*(continued on page 46)*

## The Marshals of the Empire

Napoleon liked to claim that every one of his soldiers carried what was potentially a marshal's baton in his backpack. While there was some exaggeration employed in the expression, it is certain that the Napoleonic armies were open to, and receptive of, talent wherever it might be found. A striking case is found in the men who were made marshals of the Empire: many of them came from humble or middle-class backgrounds.

Between 1804 and 1815, 26 men were raised to the rank of marshal of the French Empire. They were, in the order of rank: Berthier, Moncey, Massena, Murat, Jordan, Augereau, Bernadotte (who later became king of Sweden), Brune, Mortier, Lannes, Soult, Ney, Davout, Kellermann, Bessieres, Perignon, Lefebvre and Serurier (all raised to marshal in 1804); Perrin (1807), Macdonald (1809), Marmont (1809), Oudinot (1809), Sucet (1811) St. Cyr (1812) Pontiatowski (1813) and Grouchy in 1815.

The marshals played a vital role in the Napoleonic armies. Napoleon was famous for his ability to size up a situation and issue the general commands. Alexander Bethier, first man raised to marshal in 1804, was Napoleon's indispensable chief of staff; Berthier issued the commands and sent post riders with dispatches to different parts of the battlefield. Once those messages were received by the different marshals, they then implemented them. It was a system that worked remarkably well from about 1796, when Napoleon first took command in Italy, until about 1810. During those 14 years, Napoleon seldom lost a major battle, and his marshals were both inspired by him, and lent confidence to the men below them.

Then something happened. The failure of several marshals in Spain weakened the confidence in the overall system, and in the Russian campaign of 1812, Napoleon seemed strangely listless.

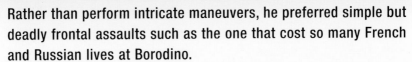

Rather than perform intricate maneuvers, he preferred simple but deadly frontal assaults such as the one that cost so many French and Russian lives at Borodino.

One brief moment of shining glory remained to Napoleon and the marshals. In the spring of 1814, as they defended the homeland of France, Napoleon and his marshals performed feat after feat of logistics and morale. With barely 200,000 men, they nearly stopped the allied 500,000. But it all came to naught when, in April, Napoleon abdicated the throne.

When King Louis XVIII returned to Paris in 1814, he announced a general amnesty for those who would swear allegiance to him. Many came forward, Marshals Ney, Massena, and Macdonald among them. The former Napoleonic marshals were treated with dignity, and given important positions in the new Bourbon army. Then came the escape from Elba.

Massena prevaricated until Napoleon was back in power. Ney told King Louis XVIII he would bring Napoleon back to Paris in a cage, but Ney then went over to his old chief. Macdonald remained loyal to the king. Most tragic of all was Marshal Berthier. Worn out from more than 30 years of campaigning, he left France and was in a German town when he fell to his death on June 1, 1815.

After the defeat at Waterloo, most of the marshals endured minor persecutions until a general amnesty was proclaimed in 1819. The major exception was Marshal Ney. The "bravest of the brave" was placed up against a wall and shot, as a reminder to any who might seek to revive the Napoleonic legend in the future.

Most fortunate of all the marshals was Bernadotte, who became King Charles XIV of Sweden in 1815. The new king pioneered a peaceful course for Sweden, which lasted through and beyond his reign.

(*continued from page 43*)

heavy casualties upon the enemies before he had been forced to abdicate. But this time would be different. Rather than wait for the coalition of Allies to surround him, Napoleon went forward to the attack.

By the first week of June, Napoleon and 110,000 Frenchmen were crossing the border from France into Belgium. They entered the Low Countries by crossing the Sambre River, and collided with Prussian forces at Charleroi.

The duchess of Richmond gave a splendid ball in Brussels on the evening of June 15. The duchess had inquired of the Duke of Wellington whether it was proper for her to do so in the situation; Wellington had replied that it was safe, proper, and good for morale. Wellington was there that night, and enjoyed himself as much as anyone until about 10 o'clock when a messenger brought news: Napoleon had crossed the Sambre and attacked the British posts near Quatre Bras. Indeed, the French assault seemed on the verge of splitting the British and Prussian armies away from each other.

Eyewitnesses later recalled that Wellington became pale and drawn. He hurried to a map room with the duke of Richmond, where Wellington exploded, "Napoleon has humbugged me, by God! He has stolen 24 hours' march on me!" That, of course, was what Napoleon had been famous for doing for the past 15 years, but the duke of Richmond did not point out the fact. Rather, he inquired where Wellington would fight the French.

First gesturing, then pointing to the map, Wellington replied, "I have ordered the army to concentrate at Quatre-Bras; but we shall not stop him there, and if so, I must fight him here," pressing his thumbnail over the position of Waterloo. Clearly, Wellington had reconnoitered well and had seen that the low hills of Mont St. Jean gave him the best chance to replicate the type of victories he had won over the French in days past in Spain. But Wellington had to make great speed to reach his rendezvous with Bonaparte.

# Quatre-Bras and Ligny

Wellington and his men hurried to the battlefield at Quatre-Bras. Napoleon had indeed "humbugged" them, and if they did not make haste, they would be completely split off from their Prussian allies. Robert Alexander Hillingford painted this portrait of the British Army in motion.

*"Perhaps the eyes of the three greatest commanders of the age were directed on one another."*

The sky was bright and clear on the morning of Friday, June 16. Three armies converged on two small villages in southern Belgium, with the fate of three nations at risk: France, Prussia, and Britain.

Having indeed stolen a march, and 24 hours on his foes, Napoleon now wanted to deal a death blow. From the beginning of the campaign, his intention had been to drive a wedge between the British and Prussian armies, and cause each of them to fall back in the direction of their supply lines. For the British that would mean an orderly retreat toward the English Channel; for the Prussians it meant a retreat toward the Rhine River. In either case, Napoleon was confident that he could choose which of his two foes to pursue, and utterly destroy him.

Up to the morning of June 16, Napoleon's maneuvers had been as close to perfect as he could have hoped. But he could not be in two places at one time; therefore Marshal Ney would lead the assault on the British at Quatre-Bras, while Napoleon would deal a heavy blow against the Prussians at Ligny.

Shown on a map, the military situation resembled a triangle. The British-Dutch forces were spread from northwest to southeast, with their southeast line anchored on Quatre-Bras. The Prussians extended more east to west, with their western line anchored at Ligny. Napoleon had cleverly come between them, and was planning blows at the connecting sections of the triangle. If he was successful, the enemy would fly off in retreat: the triangle would not hold.

Napoleon planned a devastating attack, based on the concept of the center. This meant that he would use his army, in the central position, to attack the two allied armies simultaneously, but that the right wing of Marshal Ney's section would swing over to Napoleon's left at midday and help complete the destruction of the Prussians. Ney's right was commanded by General d'Erlon.

Before the battle began, the Duke of Wellington rode to the Prussian lines to assure Marshal Blücher that the British would come to his aid. As he arrived, the duke witnessed the heart of the Prussian army being led onto the slopes that faced south, toward the enemy. This deployment ran contrary to everything the duke had practiced in India and Spain; he urged Blücher to alter the disposition, and to place the men on the reverse slope, where they would be protected from French cannon fire. Blücher declined to do so, perhaps because the French were about to begun their assault.

A Prussian lieutenant colonel, standing close to Wellington and Blücher, observed that "in the distance a party of the enemy, and Napoleon was clearly distinguishable in the group. Perhaps the eyes of the three greatest commanders of the age were directed on one another."

Wellington rode back to his own lines. Long before he reached them, he heard cannon fire in his rear. The twin battles of Ligny and Quatre-Bras had begun.

Much as historians like to praise Marshal Ney ("bravest of the brave"), there is no doubt he let Napoleon down on the 16th of June. The British-Dutch at Quatre-Bras numbered only about 8,000 men, but Ney was uncharacteristically cautious that morning. Conferring with his staff, Ney voiced the opinion that Quatre-Bras might be a "Spanish-type battle" with the best British troops ensconced on the other side of a hill. Fearful over Wellington's tactical skill, Ney waited until two in the afternoon before launching his assault.

Napoleon meanwhile, had waited until he heard the thunder of cannon from the west, indicating that Ney had begun his attack. Napoleon's forces turned on the Prussians with a savage attack, but were met by the Prussians who fought with vigor and determination. All afternoon the battle raged back and forth, with the French often gaining ground, but usually yielding some of it to cavalry counterattacks. Blücher himself led one of the Prussian cavalry charges.

The 72-year-old marshal led his Hussars in a downhill charge against the French. As he neared the bottom

This cavalry officer is typical of those Imperial Guardsmen who made the charge that won the Battle of Ligny, late in the afternoon. In campaigns fought across the continent, the Imperial Guard had never been known to retreat once it was committed to battle.

of the hill, Blücher had his horse shot from beneath him, and the aged marshal wound up just feet from being trampled to death by his own cavalry. But cooler heads saved the day, and Blücher was hurried to the back of the Prussian lines, not a moment too soon.

If personal valor could have won the day at Ligny, then Blücher and the Prussians deserved to win, but Napoleon had plans and counterplans ready for them. The battle was still a rough stalemate at about six that evening, when Napoleon sent in 14 battalions of the Imperial Guard against the enemy.

Imperial Guardsmen were tall men, capped with bearskin hats. They tended to be drawn from all the other regiments after being cited for bravery and skill. Once a man entered the Imperial Guard, which was divided into the Young Guard, Middle Guard, and Old Guard, he did not hope for a peaceful retirement. Like the Sioux warriors of the Great Plains of North America, Imperial Guardsmen expected to die on the battlefield.

The Imperial Guard swept over the Prussians like a firestorm, breaking their last defenses. The battle was won by seven o'clock, and had Napoleon committed his entire army to the chase, the Prussians might have been finished off that night. But both sides had taken heavy losses (12,000 French casualties and 16,000 Prussian) and Napoleon was ready to celebrate his victory. One leg of the allied triangle had been forced and its members sent off in retreat.

Because Blücher was temporarily out of commission, leadership of the Prussian army fell to his chief of staff, Gnesieau. Few generals and chiefs of staff worked together as well as these two, but they had decidedly different thoughts about the state of the campaign. Worried over his supply lines, Gnesieau wanted to retreat towards the Prussian lines at Liege, which would do exactly what Napoleon had set out to accomplish. Gneseaiu had the temporary command, but when Blücher came to, he insisted the Prussian retreat be north, towards Wavre. By heading in that direction, the Prussians retreated on a line parallel to Wellington and the British, as they marched toward Mont St. Jean.

Not only had Marshal Ney commenced his attack at two o'clock in the afternoon; he had countermanded an order from Napoleon which had disastrous effects upon the French plans.

From the start, Napoleon's plan had been to use the central position to throw men as a fulcrum against the Prussian left. General d'Erlon's corps, which formed the right flank of Ney's force, had been ordered to do this and had actually started marching when Marshal Ney countermanded the order and required them to return to Quatre-Bras. Furious, Napoleon sent another set of orders but it was too late. D'Erlon's corps, which might have provided the finishing blow either at Quatre-Bras or at Ligny, was available to neither Ney nor Napoleon. What might have been a stunning French victory turned into a draw at Quatre-Bras and an incomplete victory over the Prussians at Ligny.

Wellington's men retired in good order and made for the hills at Mont St. Jean. Perhaps they had been knocked about by Ney's attacks, but it was nothing like what the Prussians had endured at Ligny.

Napoleon rose early on the morning of June 17. He spent two hours inspecting the previous day's battle-field. What he saw convinced Napoleon that his plan had succeeded. By occupying the central position, and striking hard at the Prussians, he had sent them flying eastward to the Rhine. He had indeed knocked the stuffing out of the Prussians the day before. Thousands of Prussian prisoners were brought forward; their muskets were taken, and they were sent to the rear.

Marshal Grouchy asked the emperor for orders, but received a brush-off. Napoleon wanted Grouchy to keep

tabs on the retreating Prussians, to harass them if necessary. But to Napoleon the situation seemed better than
it really was. Thinking that the Prussians would retire
due east, he thought he could now give all his attention
to the British.

Napoleon began his pursuit of the British at midday.
The French now had the advantage of numbers and
momentum; the Anglo-Dutch forces were in an orderly
but clear retreat to the north. Had Napoleon and Ney
been able to fall upon them in the retreat, the French
might have wrecked havoc on their foe, but Napoleon
and Ney could not work miracles. They made slow but
steady progress that day, and in the late afternoon came
a series of powerful thunderstorms that delayed the
French further. Clearly, the momentous battle would
have to wait for at least one night.

Meanwhile, Wellington had led the Anglo-Dutch
troops to a series of gentle slopes in an area called Mont St.
Jean, about two miles south of the duke's headquarters,
which were in a small hamlet called Waterloo.

Wellington had carefully chosen this ground. He
knew that morale would plummet if Napoleon entered
Brussels, it was necessary to stop him here. The duke had
chosen a fine defensive position. The low ridges around
Mont St. Jean afforded his men protection from French
cannon fire; his army stood astride the crossroads of the
two roads intersecting in the town; and there were two
manmade obstacles in the way of any French assault: a
chateau and a farm, each of which could be garrisoned by
Anglo-Dutch troops.

The only significant drawback to Wellington's position
was that retreat would be hazardous at best. Only one road
led away to the north, and just two miles north of Mont St.
Jean it passed through the town of Waterloo. Just beyond
Waterloo lay the Forest of Soignes which would make a

Field Marshal von Blücher lost his horse, and nearly his life, in the evening at the Battle of Quatre-Bras. The old cavalry commander impulsively led a charge of his Prussian dragoons, and was nearly killed when his horse was shot from under him. Had Blücher perished, the outcome of the campaign might have been quite different.

mass exodus nearly impossible. For this reason, some planners believed Wellington had made a mistake, but there was some precedent for his action. In 1781, during the American Revolution, General Daniel Morgan had arranged his men in a defensive line at Cowpens, North Carolina, with a river directly at their back. Their pursuer, Colonel Banastre Tarleton, had risked everything on a frontal assault, and had been completely broken by the mixture of militiamen and Continental soldiers under

Morgan. Cowpens had been one of the shortest (one hour), bloodiest (for the British), and decisive battles of the Revolutionary War.

Whether or not he knew of Cowpens, Wellington had chosen the ground and would make his stand on the gentle slopes of Mont St. Jean.

# First Phase

Drawing by W. Heath shows British and French soldiers fighting during the Battle of Waterloo near a farm-house known as "La Haye Sainte."

*"Had it not rained on the night of the 17th of June, 1815, the future of Europe would have been changed. A few drops of water more or less prostrated Napoleon. That Waterloo should be the end of Austerlitz, Providence needed only a little rain, and an unseasonable cloud crossing the sky sufficed for the overthrow of the world."*

Victor Hugo, *Les Miserables*

The 18th of June was a Sunday. Light dawned over soggy, wet soldiers on all three sides. British troops rose early and went to breakfast over the fields at Mont St. Jean; French soldiers did the same not one mile to the south; and Prussians packed up nearly eight miles away at Wavre. The armies of three nations were ready for the most important day in their campaign.

Napoleon breakfasted with a group of officers at a farm called Le Caillou. From this, his headquarters, Napoleon could see the allied defenses, just atop the nearby ridge, and could make his estimate of them. But Napoleon waited to hear from his top officers.

Marshal Soult, who had fought the British in Spain, suggested the French might maneuver to force Wellington off his defensive line on the ridge. Other officers cautiously put forth the same opinion, to which Napoleon replied:

"Because Wellington has beaten you, you think he is a great general. I tell you Wellington is a bad general, the English are bad troops, and this affair will be no more difficult than eating one's breakfast." The emperor proceeded to eat his potato and eggs, and his officers scattered to their posts. Napoleon had spoken; there was nothing more to be said.

One mile to the north, the Duke of Wellington made his preparations in solitude. One of the characteristic aspects of the duke's leadership was that he surveyed the ground beforehand, made his decisions, and handed them out to subordinates without much discussion of the matter. Like Napoleon, Wellington was a supreme egotist, confident in his superior mental powers. But unlike Napoleon, Wellington had the good grace not to appear that way in public.

Only eight miles to the east, Field Marshal von Blücher and 70,000 Prussians began making their way toward the fields of Waterloo. The ground was soft and wet, the wagons would not make it through the mud so the exasperated Prussians had to haul virtually all the equipment by hand.

Somewhere south and east of the Prussians was French Marshal Grouchy with 33,000 men. He had lost contact with the bulk of the Prussian army, and by now he realized that the Prussians were somewhere between him and Napoleon—a very dangerous situation. Dispatch riders were quickly sent to Napoleon, who would receive the bad news around 12 o'clock noon.

On the fields of Waterloo, Napoleon delayed the French attack for two hours. He wanted the ground to dry out and become firm, so the French cannon balls would take their maximum effect on the enemy lines. On dry ground, cannon balls bounced and sprayed, taking immense toll on enemy lines. But in the mud, as on the morning of June 18, cannon balls came to an abrupt stop limiting their effectiveness. Napoleon was also unaware that Wellington had already taken important precautions. Many of the allied troops were lined up on the reverse side of the ridges, so they would not be harmed by cannon fire. Wellington would not be drawn into the type of trap that Blücher had stumbled into at the Battle of Ligny.

During the late morning, Napoleon held a grand review of his army, in full view of the Anglo-Dutch foe. French battalions marched and countermarched; bearskin caps were in evidence; and the bands played "Partant pour la Syrie!" (Leaving for Syria!).

The Battle of Waterloo began at about 20 minutes past 11 that morning. A thunder of French cannon was heard, and powder and shot began to spray from both armies. The final decision had been made; the battle was on.

In between the French and allied positions lay a chateau named Hougoumont and a farm called La Haye Sainte. The chateau lay on the French left; the farm was on their right. Napoleon knew that both these positions were important, but he judged the chateau as of more consequence, and the first wave of French infantry attacked La Hougoumont at half-past 11 o'clock.

Colonel Macdonnell commanded the British defenders of the chateau. So fiercely did the British fight that what seemed as if it should fall within one hour took all afternoon. Napoleon's younger brother Prince Jerome was one of the thousands of French troops who milled about the Chateau, firing at the windows, but were unable to force the issue. Once, an immense French sergeant, aptly named "The Enforcer," pushed his way through the main gate, but he and the men who followed him were killed instantly by British musket fire. For the moment, the Chateau held.

Just before he launched the central part of his attack, Napoleon caught a glimpse of dust four miles to his right. His experienced eye had noticed something that his marshals and generals had not. When he called upon Soult and others to confer, they tended to dismiss it as an act of nature (a dust storm), but Napoleon knew better. The wet conditions of the previous night would not permit such a freak of nature; it had to be a column of troops. What neither Napoleon nor his staff could determine was the nationality of those men. The French leaders hoped it was Marshal Grouchy and his 33,000 men, but Napoleon knew it was unlikely the marshal could have advanced so far that morning. The likelihood was that it was the Prussian enemy.

It was Prussians indeed, General Bulow's corps, which formed the advanced part of Blücher's army.

All morning, Marshal Blücher had incessantly

admonished and encouraged his men. They *must* reach the battlefield in time to assist Wellington. No matter that the road was soaked from the previous night's rain, or that the men were exhausted from two days of fighting and marching. They must reach the duke on the heights of Mont St. Jean.

At one o'clock in the afternoon, Napoleon launched the central part of his attack. The corps commanded by Count Drouet d'Erlon advanced up the middle part of the slope, with the chateau to their left and the farm on their right. It was a mass of infantry, marching in their traditional columns, with the men shouting "Vive l'Empereur." Any of the British and Dutch defenders who had not previously faced the French must have been quite affected by the shouts.

One of the British soldiers prepared to receive this assault was Captain James Mercer of the Royal Artillery. Not long after the battle, he composed a memoir which is considered one of the single best accounts of Waterloo. As a disclaimer, Mercer penned the following lines:

A scientific relation of this great struggle, on which the fate of Europe hinged, I pretend not to write. I write neither history, nor 'Memoirs pour servir a l'Histoire,' etc. etc., but only pure gossip for my own simple amusement—just what happened to me and mine, and what I did see happen to other about me. Depend upon it, he who pretends to give a general account of a great battle from his own observation deceives you—believe him not. He can see no farther (that is, if he be personally engaged in it) than the length of his nose; and how it he to tell what is pass-ing two or three miles off, with hills and trees and buildings intervening, and all enveloped in smoke?

Marshal Blücher encourages his men to make haste as they move to join Wellington and the British. Though the 72-year-old Blücher had taken a fall at the Battle of Ligny, he was back in the saddle, and only he could push his Prussian troops to make the effort to reach the British in time to prevent a Napoleonic victory.

What Mercer did see, and what he and his fellows experienced, was the force of the French assault. These were veterans of many battles, men who had been tried and tested in the French column strategy.

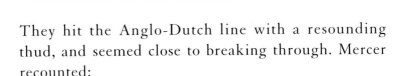
They hit the Anglo-Dutch line with a resounding thud, and seemed close to breaking through. Mercer recounted:

> It might have been about two o'clock when Colonel Gould, R. A., came to me, perhaps a little later. Be that as it may, we were conversing on the subject of our situation, which appeared to him rather desperate. He remarked that in the event of a retreat, there was but one road, which no doubt would be instantly choked up, and asked my opinion. My answer was, 'It does indeed look very bad; but I trust in the duke, who, I am sure, will get us out of it somehow or other.' Meantime, gloomy reflections arose in my mind, for though I did not choose to betray myself (as we spoke before the men), yet I could not help thinking that our affairs were rather desperate, and that some unfortunate catastrophe was at hand. In this case I made up my mind to spike my guns and retreat over the fields, draught-horses and all, in the best manner I could, steering well from the highroad and general line of retreat.

Things looked black for the allied army until someone gave an order to four brigades of British cavalry. It is unclear today whether Lord Ponsonby gave the order or whether the duke sent a message, but suddenly about 2,400 British and Scottish horsemen came over the ridge and crashed into the French lines, wielding sabers.

Normally, European infantry—whether they were British, French, or other—knew how to repel a cavalry charge. On an order, the infantry would form a hollow square and use musket fire and bayonets to stop the foe. But there was no time to form squares; d'Erlon's men had crested the ridge in column formation, and they were too compacted already to change their formation. For one of the few times in the Napoleonic Wars, a cavalry assault had a large body of infantry at its mercy.

The British and Scottish cavalrymen did their work efficiently and with a vengeance. In less than half an hour they mauled d'Erlon's infantry. Two thousand French were taken prisoner and two Napoleonic eagles were seized by the British. Just half an hour after cresting the ridge, the remains of d'Erlon's men were back in the lowland between the two lines in full retreat.

Again, no one knows who gave the order, but the allied cavalrymen took up the shout, "Scotland forever!" and charged after the retreating foe. So sudden was the charge, and so demoralized were the French that the cavalry caught up with the foe and reached the ridge where 70 of Napoleon's prized cannon lay. The cavalrymen gleefully began to spike the guns, and any neutral observer—there actually were none—might have thought the day was won for the allied army.

Napoleon struck back. He had 30,000 men held in reserve, but it only took sudden charges by his own cavalry to send the allied horsemen reeling. The British and Scottish horses were winded from their exertions; the French mounts were fresh and eager. Within 15 minutes, the gallant Allies cavalry was sent back to its own slopes, with about half of the number that it had begun the action. But the cavalry intervention had been crucial; d'Erlon's assault had been broken and the left center of the allied lines had withstood.

Direction of the French attack now shifted to Marshal Michel Ney, who commanded the French left and whose men were still battling furiously in an effort to capture the Chateau of Hougoumont. By this time, over 10,000 Frenchmen had been drawn into what should have been a sideshow to the main effort.

Michel Ney, the son of a cooper (barrel maker), was indeed "the bravest of the brave." His performance at Waterloo was marred by a series of impulsive decisions, brought on perhaps by the incredible stress and fatigue he had suffered in the Russian campaign two and a half years earlier.

# Second Phase

*"None of your furious galloping charges was this, but a deliberate advance, at a deliberate pace, as of men resolved to carry their point."*

Captain James Mercer

Time had shown—and Waterloo would prove once more—that Michel Ney was indeed the "bravest of the brave." The son of a cooper, Ney was born in 1769, the same year as Napoleon and Wellington. He had joined the French hussars in 1788, and then become a soldier in the Revolutionary armies. He had been one of the first marshals of the Empire, created in 1804. Ney had fought brilliantly in the 1805 campaign that culminated in Napoleon's greatest victory at Austerlitz. He had fought gallantly, but without success, against Wellington in Spain. More than anything else, though, men remembered Ney's bravery in the terrible campaign in Russia during 1812-1813. There had been times when Ney and a handful of elite grenadiers had stopped whole Russian units at bridges, thereby allowing the main part of the retreating French army to escape. Throughout that terrible winter, Ney had braved death time and again; bullets seemed to miss him when they should have skewered him. Now, on June 18th, Ney directed the left center of the French lines and Napoleon allowed him a free hand in his dispositions.

Furious over what he had witnessed of d'Erlon's repulse, Ney ordered his own cannon to redouble their bombardment of the allied lines. Here, the French cannon took a heavy toll of the Anglo-Dutch defenders, and by about three o'clock, Ney saw something that made him catch his breath; he witnessed British troops being marched to the rear and replaced by fresher units.

This type of rearrangement was Wellington's specialty. The duke understood the value of rotating his men in position, and as a consequence, his men were often able to deliver a greater performance. Seeing the toll taken by the French bombardment, Wellington now undertook one of his classic shifts.

Ney, who had fought against Wellington in the past, should have seen this movement for what it was. But throughout the battle, Ney displayed a fury that overrode his thinking. Seeing the British withdraw led to a feeling of elation. Ney believed the allied line was quivering, and that one decisive smashing blow would yield the result for which he longed. Acting quickly, he summoned his entire cavalry reserve, roughly 5,000 men, forward.

They made the most spectacular sight yet seen that

day. There were French cuirassiers and Polish lancers, brightly outfitted and shiny. Of the three sections of the army (infantry, artillery, cavalry) the horsemen were by far the most dramatic in appearance. Napoleon had always had a good cavalry, but in his campaigns in Poland he had recruited Polish lancers who had added to the size and splendor of his mounted horse brigades. What they were about to engage in was more reminiscent of medieval warfare than the 19th century.

Led by Ney himself, the French cavalry moved up the slope toward the waiting British. The French came on not with a rush, but at a canter, and Captain Mercer, still with his cannon, recounted what he saw:

> We were still talking on this subject, when suddenly a dark mass of cavalry appeared for an instant on the main ridge, and then came sweeping down the slope in swarms, reminding me of an enormous surf bursting over the prostrate hull of a stranded vessel, and then running, hissing and foaming, up the beach. The hollow space became in a twinkling covered with horsemen, crossing, turning, and riding about in all directions, apparently without any object. Sometimes they would come near us, then would return a little. There were lancers amongst them, hussars and dragoons—it was a complete melee.

From his position, Mercer could not see the infantry squares quickly form on the crest of the ridge. As the French and Polish horsemen came over the top, they saw British infantry drawn up in hollow squares, with musket and bayonet pointed outward.

The cavalry charged the squares. Fire and smoke bellowed from the squares, and dozens of mounts lost their riders in a matter of seconds. No matter, the horsemen

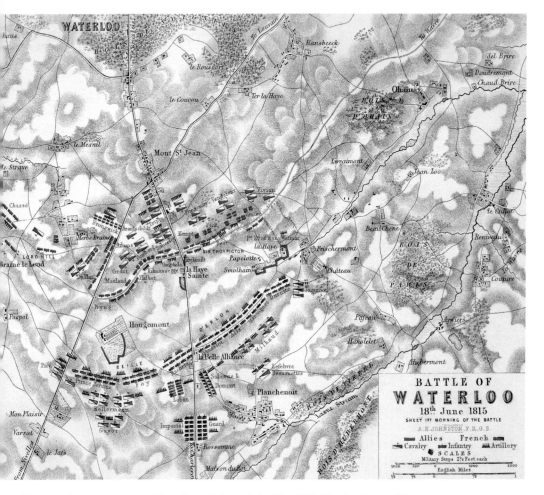

The battle was approaching its crisis point. All of Wellington's positions still held, but the Chateau Hougoumont would eventually fall, and there was a real possibility that Napoleon would unleash the Imperial Guard who might sweep the entire British position as they had done to the Prussians at Ligny.

charged round and round the British squares, seeking a breakthrough. Perhaps 10 minutes elapsed before Michel Ney led his horsemen off the ridge and back to the plateau.

Half a mile off, at La Belle Alliance, Napoleon observed the charge with consternation. It was unheard of for a commander to loose his cavalry upon infantry unless he had infantry or artillery support of his own. Turning to Marshal Soult, Napoleon commented:

"This is a precipitate action that may ruin the day. It comes an hour too early, but we must support what has been done." Kellerman's infantry was ordered forward to support Ney's cavalry.

Why did Napoleon not act to reverse Ney's commands? This has been one of the most debated questions of the Waterloo battle. The first cavalry charge had occurred without any consultation, and could not be halted, but surely Napoleon could have prevented any further such actions. Instead he glowered into his field glass and let the action continue.

Aside from the unlikely idea that Napoleon had lost his gift for command, two possible answers present themselves. First, the emperor was not well. He suffered from hemorrhoids and stomach cramps, and seemed particularly unwell that day. Second, perhaps more important, his mind was diverted by the increasing sound of gunfire to his extreme left, the east. Blue Prussian uniforms were starting to emerge from the woods, and cause Napoleon grave concern. They were still two miles away, but their position threatened to undo all he had planned.

Whatever the reason, Napoleon stayed his hand and allowed Ney to determine events on the center left of the battlefield. As he came down from the ridge that first time, Michel Ney must have had some doubts as to whether he could break those solid infantry squares. But issuing a challenge of that type was like waving a red flag in front of the man who had dared death a dozen times in the Russian campaign. Ney waited only a few minutes, reformed his cavalry, and charged up once more.

What followed was an exact repeat of what went before. The French gained the ridge, came over the crest, and milled about in the center of the British infantry squares. Here and there a cavalryman managed to reach a line, to hack with his saber, but most of the casualties were French. Riders and mounts fell everywhere. Again, the words of Captain Mercer:

> The column now once more mounted the plateau, and these popping gentry wheeled off right and left to clear the ground for their charge. The spectacle was imposing, and if ever the word sublime was appropriately applied, it might surely be to it. On they came in compact squadrons, one behind the other, so numerous that those of the rear were still below the brow when the head of the column was but some 60 or 70 yards from our guns. Their pace was a slow but steady trot. None of your furious galloping charges was this, but a deliberate advance, at a deliberate pace, as of men resolved to carry their point.

No one knows exactly how many times the French cavalry charged that afternoon. Estimates run as high as 12 charges, some as low as eight. In either case, Ney and the cavalry established without the slightest doubt both their courage and the futility of their attacks. By five o'clock, the French cavalry was a spent force. Those men and horses who remained alive had no energy left to give to the battle.

Back at La Belle Alliance, Napoleon saw a battle scene that gave him deep concern. The Prussians were forcing back his right flank more by the minute, and the village of Placenoit had fallen to their advance. Prussian cannon near the village were sending round shot that crashed around Napoleon's encampment, and it looked as if any type of

Marshal Ney led his cavalrymen in charge after charge up the slopes. Three horses were killed under him, but the relentless Ney continued to pound at the enemy.

retreat he might envision would be thwarted. From his vantage point, Napoleon witnessed the wreckage of his magnificent cavalry, and the continued fruitless efforts of Marshal Ney. It was time for a decision.

To disengage would be discouraging to his men, disheartening to his cause. Napoleon decided to fight the battle out. He sent for the leaders of the Young Guard.

La Marseillaise was the theme song of the French Revolution and is today the French National Anthem. First sung in 1792, the song inspired its listeners to fight for the Motherland against the monarchical armies of Prussia, Austria, and Britain. Ironically, La Marseillaise was also used by Napoleon, who had himself become an Emperor.

# Third Phase

*"Up Maitland, now's your time!"*

Duke of Wellington

The Imperial Guard was the core of the Napoleonic Army. Composed strictly of hardy veterans of his earlier campaigns, the Imperial Guard was divided into three sections: the Old Guard, the Young Guard, and the Middle Guard. As expected, the "Old Guard" was composed of those who had fought with Napoleon the longest. Among their leaders was Baron Cambronne, who had accompanied the emperor into exile on Elba. The Middle Guard was composed of men who had served with distinction over the past five or six years, and the Young Guard was made up of the most promising of the younger soldiers in Napoleon's army.

Seeing how Ney was blocked by the British infantry, and that the Prussians threatened to overwhelm his right, Napoleon ordered in three battalions of the Middle Guard. True to form, those trusty soldiers swept into the village of Plancenoit and evicted three times their number of Prussians in record time. By six o'clock, the situation on Napoleon's right had stabilized enough that he could examine the situation with a clear head.

Just then, a messenger arrived from Marshal Ney, asking for more troops with which to push home the attack on Mont St. Jean. Despite the horrific losses experienced by his cavalry, Marshal Ney had continued the attacks with cannon fire and infantry attacks, and once more he believed he was on the verge of breaking through the Anglo-Dutch foe. The message asked for more men to push home the final blow.

All the chroniclers of Waterloo agree that Napoleon frowned in a most awful manner and answered: "Troops? Where does he expect me to find them? Does he think I can make them?" The answer, in the negative, was sent to Marshal Ney.

The "Bravest of the Brave" had made numerous mistakes during the battle and during the entire campaign. This once though, he probably had it right. Wellington's center and left center were crumbling under the pounding of French guns, and one determined effort with all the French reserves would probably have carried the hill and the day. Napoleon, however, aware of Ney's earlier miscalculations, was not ready to entrust his Imperial Guard to the marshal; Napoleon waited between half an hour and 45 minutes before he decided to commit his last reserve to the battle.

During that half hour, Wellington rearranged his troops for the last time. Believing that the final attack would come slightly left of center (from the French view), Wellington placed about 3,000 grenadiers there under command of General Peregrine Maitland.

At nearly seven o'clock, Napoleon led nine battalions of the Old Guard forward. He left three battalions of the Middle Guard at La Belle Alliance, and one battalion of the Old Guard to fend off any threat from Plancenoit, but the rest, all 4,500 of them, he led forward. Napoleon marched at their head until he met Marshal Ney outside of Chateau Hougoumont, which had finally fallen about an hour earlier. There, in front of the Chateau, Napoleon remained with his staff while the Guard filed past him. They were silent, the men of the Guard, and their silence betokened a savage desire to overcome the foe. At the last moment, as they approached the ridge, the Guardsmen were informed, "Soldiers, here comes Grouchy!" Hands were pointed to a cloud of dust which actually betokened the close arrival of Field Marshal von Blücher and the rest of the Prussian army. It mattered not to the men of the Guard who made their quiet march up the slope.

Waiting on the other side were the Duke of Wellington and about 3,000 well-concealed British troops, commanded by Major General Peregrine Maitland. Born in Hampshire County, England, in 1777, Maitland was an experienced leader of the Grenadier Guards. Wellington and Maitland both knew what was coming. Even if their experienced eyes had not caught the telltale signs of French columns, a French deserter had arrived breathlessly minutes before with the word that Napoleon and the Imperial Guard were on their way.

Four thousand five hundred Frenchmen were in those columns, but due to their depth, only about 300 of them actually crested the ridge at the same moment. At that very second, the duke cried out, "Up Maitland,

*La Marseillaise*, also known as the Departure of the Army in 1792, is also the name for a relief sculpture by Rude that appears on the front of the Arc de Triomphe in Paris.

now's your time!" and 3,000 British soldiers leaped up from their positions. Three thousand muskets fired as one, and the first line of Imperial Guardsmen disappeared in a cloud of smoke.

Had the Imperial Guard been able to form into ranks

on that plateau, and fight their foes one-to-one, the contest might have been equal. Instead, the Guards were simply blown away by the concentrated British musket fire. For nearly five minutes, the Imperial Guard stood and received the worst punishment it had ever endured from any foe, and then, remarkably, the Imperial Guard wavered and broke. Minutes later, Napoleon's best troops were in full retreat down the ridge, and those who could spare a look to the east could see that those men approaching were blue-coated Prussians, intent on their destruction. Grouchy had never materialized.

It was about quarter to eight in the evening. An hour of daylight remained. The Duke of Wellington took off and waved his hat, the sign for a general advance all along the line. By eight o'clock, the situation on the battlefield had become the complete reverse of one hour earlier. The French were in full flight, pursued by exhausted British and Dutch troops, and energetic and vengeful Prussians.

As bad as things were for France, things might have been even worse. The early cry of "Le Guard recule!" (The Guard retreats!) was followed by the more disastrous "Save qui peut!" (Every man for himself!). The entire French army might have been cut to pieces were it not for the heroic stand of three battalions of the Old Guard on the road by La Belle Alliance.

Led by Baron Cambronne, the three battalions formed squares and performed feats as heroic as those of the British infantry earlier in the day. Three battalions of the Old Guard held the road, and the Anglo-Dutch army for nearly an hour, while Napoleon, his staff, and some 40,000 survivors made their way to relative safety.

British voices called on the Guard to yield: "Brave

There is no denying that Arthur Wellesley, the Duke of Wellington, was cool and collected in battle. Part of the mystique that grew up around him was from his imperturbable appearance. Here he rallies his men for the last, supreme effort at the Battle of Waterloo.

Frenchmen, surrender!" Baron Cambronne gave the answer, "La Guarde meurt et ne se rend pas" (The Guard dies, but does not surrender).

Blücher and the Duke of Wellington met in front of La Belle Alliance between nine and 10 o'clock that night.

The Prussian suggested that La Belle Alliance would make an excellent name for the battle, but Wellington already had his own thoughts on the matter. Throughout the long war in Spain, the duke had made a practice of naming battles after the place where his headquarters was, and from which he wrote his final dispatches. This would be no exception. Although the battle was fought on the slopes around the village of Mont St. Jean, and although there were other, colorful names available (Hougoumont, La Belle Alliance, and La Haye Sainte all come to mind), Wellington named the battle for the hamlet of Waterloo, two miles north of the battle site.

Prussians joined with a regiment of Highlanders and sang "Heil dir im Siegerkranz," which was to the melody of "God Save the King." The opening lines are:

> Heil dir im Siegerkranz
> Herrscher des Vaterlands!
> Heil Konig, dir!
> Fuhl in des Thrones Glanz
> Die hohe Wonne ganz
> Liebling des Volkszusein
> Heil Konig, dir.

> (Hail to you in the victor's crown
> Lord of the Fatherlands
> Hail to you Leader
> From your splendid throne, feel
> The total high rapture
> For you are loved by the People
> Hail to you, Leader.)

As things turned out, Blücher had more important things to do than quarrel over names. Fifty years as a cavalryman had taught Blücher the importance of following up a victory with speed and decision. What was more,

The Duke of Wellington and Field Marshal Blücher meet in front of La Belle Alliance late in the evening. Blücher suggests that the farmhouse name be given to the Battle, but Wellington had made a practice of naming battles from the location of his headquarters, which gave the name "Waterloo" to the battle.

his Prussian soldiers ached for revenge for what had happened at Ligny three days earlier. The whole of the 19th and much of the 20th of June were spent in full pursuit by the Prussians, attempting to run down and kill French soldiers in retreat.

## Battle Songs

Songs and ballads have long been important in military history. Where would the early American military have been without "Yankee Doodle," or the British Navy without "Hail, Britannia!" The Hundred Days campaign and the Battle of Waterloo were no exceptions to the general rule; in fact, the French, Prussians, and British men may have sung even more than most armies, due to the recent innovations in military bands and parades.

The primary British song was "God Save the King." Written by Henry Carey, it had first been performed in 1745, the year that Bonnie Prince Charlie invaded Scotland and attempted to overthrow King George II. 1745 was, incidentally, also the year that the Brown Bess musket became standard equipment for British infantrymen; it remained so through the Napoleonic years.

Prussians had a wealth of songs and ballads to use, because the uprising against Napoleon in 1813 and 1814 had created an immense body of poetry, prose, and song concerning the German people and their destiny. One of the most popular German songs was "Heil dir im Siegerkranz" (Hail to You, the One with Garlands), but there were many others, including a number written by Prussian poets who took up soldiering for a time. Foremost among these was Korner, who died at the Battle of Liepzig in 1813, but whose journal and song record became venerated shortly after his death.

The French had one song that took precedence over all others. "La Marseillaise" is both one of the most dramatic and chilling of all national songs; to hear it makes one feel inspired and endangered at the same time. First sung around 1792, it represents the fury and terror of the French Revolution during its early years.

The Anglo-Dutch army, by contrast, needed rest. As Wellington said later to friends, "Never did I see such a pounding match." Veterans of the duke's Spanish campaigns, and even Napoleonic veterans of campaigns in Prussia and Russia claimed they had never witnessed such a shocking display of violence in one compact day. Waterloo dwarfed even Borodino, in Russia, three years before.

# The Aftermath

Napoleon fled into the night as his army dissolved on the battlefield. Never before had the Emperor been so badly beaten; this would be the last of forty battles.

*"Our capital is intoxicated with joy."*

Berlin newspaper, June 1815

**N**ews of Waterloo reached London four days after the battle:

The Duke of Wellington's Dispatch, dated Waterloo the 19th of June, states, that on the preceding day Buonoparte (*sic*) attacked with his whole force, the British line, supported by a corps of Prussians; which attack, after a long and sanguinary conflict, terminated in the complete Overthrow of the Enemy's Army, with the loss of 150 pieces of cannon and two eagles. During the night, the Prussians under

Marshal Blücher, who joined in the pursuit of the enemy, captured sixty guns, and a large part of Buonaparte's (*sic*) Baggage. The allied armies continue to pursue the enemy. Two French generals were taken.

Such is the great and glorious result of those masterly movements by which the Hero of Britain frustrated the audacious attempt of the Rebel Chief. Glory to Wellington, to our gallant Soldiers, and to our brave Allies! Buonaparte's (*sic*) reputation has been wrecked, and his last grand stake has been lost in this tremendous conflict. Two hundred and ten pieces of cannon captured in a single battle, put to the blush the boasting column of the Place de Vendome. Long and sanguinary, indeed, we fear, the conflict must have been; but the boldness of the Rebel Frenchmen was the boldness of despair, and conscience sat heavy on those arms which were raised against their Sovereign, against their oaths, and against the peace and happiness of their country. We confidently anticipate a great and immediate defection from the rebel cause.

*The London Times*, Thursday, June 22, 1815

Reports of the battle reached Berlin on June 24.

Our capital is intoxicated with joy. The previous news of the first attack of Napoleon, and of the undecisive actions of the 15th and 16th, of course, as in a large city, spread considerable alarm; so much the greater, therefore, was the exultation of to-day, when Lieutenant Nernst brought the glorious dispatches from Prince Blücher. He was preceeded by 30 postilions blowing their horns, and surrounded by an immense population.

Prince Blücher, we understand, has written that even the battle of Leipsic can scarcely be compared to that of the 18th of June. At the departure of the Courier, 23,000 Frenchmen lay on the field of battle. Our loss, also, was not inconsiderable. Colonel Count Schwerin was among the killed. Generals Thieleman, Jurgas, Kraft, Holzegdorfz, and Colonel Watzendorff were wounded.

Lieutenant Nernst made his journey in the captured carriage of the duke of Bassano. Besides Buonaparte's (*sic*) carriage, seven other carriages were captures. The Prussian soldiers who made this boast were laden with Napoleon's d'or.

> Berlin newspaper, translated and
> quoted by *The London Times*

The speed with which Napoleon's army disintegrated was remarkable. At seven o'clock he seemed ready to punch through with the Imperial Guard and win another great victory. At eight o'clock, his Guards reeled under the impact of musket fire from Maitland's Grenadiers. At nine o'clock, Cambronne and three battalions of Imperial Guardsmen were all that stood firm of the French army. By ten o'clock, Cambronne and his men had perished, and what was a defeat became an utter rout.

Blücher had been a cavalryman for about 55 years. He knew the importance of following up a win with a powerful pursuit. All that night and well into the next morning, Prussian cavalrymen chased French foot soldiers, cutting them down in fields, on roads, even pulling them out of trees they had climbed. What had been the most devastating loss of Napoleon's career now became an utter catastrophe, with no semblance of order or discipline remaining to his men. The morning of June 19th showed

British and Prussian soldiers entered Paris early in July. The victors conducted themselves well enough that the Parisians, while not welcoming them, received them cordially. The Napoleonic Wars had cost many Frenchmen their lives, and many people were delighted to see the end of many years of war.

a battlefield of corpses, and the dispositions of three armies. Wellington's Anglo-Dutch men remained on the field at Mont St. Jean; the Prussians were scattered everywhere in a mass pursuit; and the French—well there hardly seemed to be an army at all. Rather there was a stream of individual refugees, in complete flight.

Not once in the history of the Napoleonic Wars had an army been so thoroughly broken in one battle. Even the Austrians and Russians had extricated themselves from the Battle of Austerlitz in better fashion than the French after Waterloo.

Why, one wonders, did the French unravel so quickly and completely? The answer is twofold. Until seven o'clock in the evening, the French army retained its composure and discipline through what had been a frightful day of pounding and casualties. When the Imperial Guard failed to break through on the ridge and was instead sent in retreat, the exhaustion of the day and the bewilderment at seeing the Guards in flight combined to undo the French resolve. Making things much worse, Blücher and his cavalrymen broke through the French right at almost the same moment that the Guard failed on the ridge, turning a defeat into a catastrophe. If there is a lesson to be drawn from the last hours of the Battle, it is that a pounding offensive *must succeed* in its late stages, or the men who attempt it will be exhausted and demoralized.

That of course begs the question: Could Napoleon have withdrawn from the battle prior to sending the Imperial Guard?

Probably not. After a day of such fierce combat, had Napoleon pulled back at six or seven o'clock, his men must have been dismayed. They might have been able to disengage, even to dig in for a defense of their own, but any thoughts of winning the campaign would have ended. Therefore, Napoleon the gambler threw his last dice, and this time they came up short. The only question was: Did the gambler have one last set of die in his pocket?

Napoleon believed so. He hastened back to Paris after the defeat, where he found over 100,000 Frenchmen under arms. The potential threat to the homeland and the capital city rallied the French in a way like no other. Napoleon hoped he could be the point around which these men could rally, but he was severely disappointed by the response of the French legislature. The Corps Legislatif, led by the aged Marquis de Lafayette, called on Napoleon to abdicate for the second and final time. Try though he might, Napoleon could not persuade them otherwise, and on June 22 he submitted his final abdication.

Knowing that Marshal Blücher and many others thought he should be shot, Napoleon hastened to the French coast, and requested permission to come aboard a British ship. He wrote an emotional letter in which he asked to come to warm himself at the fireside of his one-time foes. The British took him aboard, but no promises were made as to what would become of him.

Meanwhile, Wellington and Blücher approached Paris. The Allies were wary in their advance, for they knew the advantage the French would hold in fighting battles on their own soil. Marshal Davout, who had proved on the of most trustworthy of the marshals, led the defense, and there was every reason to expect a bloodbath as the Allies attempted to force the city.

Surprisingly, a convention or armistice was reached on July 3. Under its terms, the French army withdrew from Paris and moved south of the Loire River, while Wellington, Blücher, and their armies moved into the city on July 6. Just one day later, King Louis XVIII arrived and took his place at the Tuileries Palace; critics charged he had arrived "in the baggage train of the allied armies."

If there is any such thing as an amicable occupation, it might be said to have been the allied occupation of Paris. Wellington, hailed by friend and foe alike, was notable for his generous approach to the defeated enemy. Blücher, on the other hand, wanted vengeance for the many humiliations Prussia had suffered after its defeat by Napoleon. Most important, Blücher intended to blow up the Pont D'Ienna

(Jena Bridge) which had been built to commemorate the French victory over the Prussians at Jena in 1806. Blücher went so far as to have explosives placed, but was stopped by a fortunate combination of the duke of Wellington and King Louis XVIII.

By the end of July 1815, the entire campaign had ended. Nearly 800,000 allied soldiers had been mobilized from the plains of Russia to the downs of England, but only about 230,000 of these—Wellington and Blücher's men—had played a real part. Between them, the British duke and the Prussian marshal had brought down the emperor and his marshals.

Napoleon's remains were entombed in the circular crypt at Les Invalides in Paris. Les Invalides began as a military hospital, and gradually became the showpiece for French military history. It stands on the south side of the Seine River.

# The Results

*"That day, the perspective of the human race changed. Waterloo is the hinge of the nineteenth century. The disappearance of the great man was necessary for the advent of the great century."*

Victor Hugo, *Les Miserables*

Time has not removed the glow, the glory, or the despair that men felt on the battlefield of Waterloo. It remains one of the most important, and among the most studied of all military subjects. Even today, the visitor can peer in the windows of the Chateau de Hougoumont, stroll by La Belle Alliance, or climb the enormous mound constructed to honor the men who fought and died there.

Was Victor Hugo correct? Did Napoleon have to disappear so that a new age and a new world could begin? Those questions too, have been discussed and debated ever since.

Napoleon was, without doubt, the most significant national leader in Europe from 1820, when he became first consul, until his defeat at Waterloo. For the six years remaining to him, he composed his memoirs, and even after his death, the Napoleonic legend grew with the passing years. To a Frenchman such as Victor Hugo, there was no doubt that Napoleon was the "great man" of his era.

But Victor Hugo published *Les Miserables* in 1862, the same year that Union and Confederate soldiers faced each other at Antietam, the year that Abraham Lincoln issued the Emancipation Proclamation. The passing of 140 years since allows us a fuller vision of Napoleon, his times, and his importance to them.

Without question, Napoleon spread the message of the French Revolution to other European nations. Though he was a dictator at home, and though he longed to impose his will on all of Europe, the ideas of Liberty, Fraternity, and Equality nevertheless went across Europe with his armies.

At the same time, Napoleon's style and attitude resembled that of King Louis XIV who said "L'Etat, c'est moi" ("I am the State"). This absolutist idea and approach belonged to the late 17th and early 18th century rather than the 19th. In terms of government, Napoleon was a throwback to an earlier time.

The overthrow of Napoleon was followed by a long period of political reaction. Conservative leaders such as Klemmens von Metternich and Czar Alexander dominated the European scene for the next generation. Not until the great revolutions of 1848 did the common people of Europe burst through to the center stage once more.

Finally we might ask: What was the result of Napoleon's career on Britain?

It would be reasonable to suppose that Britain might be exhausted and weakened by 20 years of struggle, but the opposite is true. The Napoleonic Wars actually enhanced Britain's standing among the nations; she enlarged her navy, her commerce, and her colonies during this period. After Waterloo, Britain stood on top of the world for the next 50 years.

So much for nations and policies. What about the leaders?

The Duke of Wellington became the toast of England, and indeed of all Europe. No British commander since the duke of Marlborough had won so many victories, and none since Marlborough had gained the trust and belief of so many of his men. Wellington had once more earned the trust shown him by Czar Alexander, who had urged him to save Europe again.

Wellington went on to become the most trusted public servant in the first half of the century. He served twice as prime minister, and was one of the most valued advisers of Queen Victoria. When he died in 1851, the British public mourned in a way that was not seen again until the death of Winston Churchill in 1965.

Prince Blücher was the toast of all Germany, and was briefly lionized in England as well. Stories spread of Blücher's legendary willpower and energy, how he had survived the fall from his horse at Ligny, and come back to complete the destruction of Napoleon. Numerous poems and songs were composed in his honor. Following Blücher's desire, the poets and songwriters wrote of Blücher and the Battle of Schönbund, the German word for "La Belle Alliance." Enormously popular at home, Blücher came to be distrusted in other countries for his vengeful approach to France and the French.

Napoleon fared poorly. He made overtures to the British government, asking to be taken in as a refugee, and given asylum in the land he had done so much to oppose, but the British government, headed by the prince regent, firmly refused. Napoleon was indeed taken aboard the British man of war *H. M. S. Bellerophon*, but he was taken first to Portsmouth, and then to the remote island of St. Helena in the south-central Atlantic Ocean. There would be no repeat of the escape from Elba.

Napoleon died on St. Helena in 1821. For many years his remains were kept there; the British feared even a return of his bones to the soil of France. But in 1840, the son of King Louis-Philippe was permitted to travel to St. Helena and bring the remains back to France. They were interred at Les Invalides in Paris, in a tremendous ceremony, and the resting site is one of the most visited places in France today.

Marshal Ney fared even worse than his chief. During the last phase of Waterloo, Ney was seen brandishing his sword and shouting, "Come and see how a marshal of France dies!" But as Victor Hugo later wrote, "Unhappy man! thou wast reserved for French bullets!" Ney was captured after the battle, and tried by the French House of Peers for treason against King Louis XVIII. Even the king lamented that Ney had been caught, but justice was served. On December 8, 1815, the prince of the Moskawa, the leader of the French throughout most of the battle of Waterloo, the Bravest of the Brave was lined up against a wall and shot.

Marshal Grouchy had failed in everything he had been assigned to during the Hundred Days, but it had not all been his fault. Remarkably, he did manage to extricate 33,000 men from the wreckage after Waterloo, and he guarded the French border for the next crucial days, preventing a full Prussian invasion. Grouchy lived until 1847.

Marshal Soult had been a failure as Napoleon's chief of staff, but then he too had been put in the wrong position. Soult was a brilliant marshal, but did not have the expertise

Napoleon spent the last six years of his life in exile on the island of St. Helena, in the middle of the South Atlantic Ocean. It was a tough ending for the former Emperor to endure, but he wrote his memoirs, and took many walks.

or the thoughtfulness which had distinguished the former marshal, Alexander Berthier. But Soult went on to become the most successful of the marshals after Napoleon's second fall. He continued as a marshal of France in the army of King Louis XVIII, King Charles X, and even King Louis Philippe. In 1847, Soult was created a marshal general of

France, a distinction achieved by only four soldiers in the long military history of France. Soult died in 1851.

General Cambronne fared better than anyone might have expected. Last seen on the battlefield at Waterloo, he had shouted "Le guard meurt and ne se rend pas." But Cambronne survived that awful night, and was taken to England as a prisoner, where he was treated with great honor. Repatriated to France, he served again in the armies of King Louis XVIII, and died in 1842 in his hometown of Nantes, on the Loire. A bronze statue was erected to him there six years later. Because of the long debate over what he had shouted that night at Waterloo, Cambronne entered the French language. Throughout the 19th century and well into the 20th, "Cambronne," meant an insult.

General Peregrine Maitland of the Grenadier Guards fared well. He married Lady Sarah Lenox just weeks after the Battle of Waterloo; she was one of the Richmond family that had thrown the ball in Brussels on June 15. Maitland served as lieutenant governor of Upper Canada (which meant Toronto and Ontario), lieutenant governor of Nova Scotia, and commander in chief of the British army in Madras. He became a full general in 1846, and died in London in 1854.

The tens of thousands of men who fought and died at Waterloo had their memorial in the form of an earthen mound, erected by the Belgian government. The men who survived, especially on the Anglo-Dutch side, were showered with honors. The French survivors did less well. They returned to a country rent by 20 years of war and the enormous sacrifices made by them and their countrymen. It is a testimony to the fortitude of the French people that the indemnity of 700,000,000 francs was paid within three years, and the armies of occupation were removed by 1818.

## Napoleon's Resting Place

Napoleon died of stomach cancer on St. Helena in 1821, six years after the Battle of Waterloo. His last words were "Chief of the army."

The Europe of 1821 was very different from what it had been in 1800 or 1810. The ideas and ideals of the French Revolution were in disrepute, and monarchs such as Czar Alexander and politicians such as Metternich the Austrian prime minister were determined not to allow any repeat of the Revolutionary or Napoleonic experience. The British government was only too happy to concur with its Continental allies, and for many years Napoleon's remains stayed on the windswept island where he had spent his last years.

France underwent yet another revolution in the summer of 1830. The Parisian crowd overthrew King Charles X, who had succeeded Louis XVIII, and many called for a new French Republic. The liberals were disappointed when the aged Marquis de Lafayette announced he favored a new, more liberal monarchy instead. Largely because of Lafayette's announcement, the Parisians accepted Louis-Philippe of the house of Orleans (cousins to the Bourbons) as their new king. He promised to rule as a citizen-king and to abide by constitutional principles.

The Napoleonic legend grew during the 1830s, and King Louis-Philippe decided to harness that legend for his own benefit. He petitioned the British government, and in 1840 received permission to bring Napoleon's remains home to France. That year, the Prince de Jonville, oldest son the King Louis-Philippe, went to St. Helena and brought back to Paris the earthly remains of Napoleon Bonaparte, which were housed at Les Invalides on the south bank of the Seine River.

Napoleon thus achieved legendary status among the French people. Among the many ironies of his career is that he was at heart a Corsican, an Italian really, though he espoused the glory of France. His tomb at Les Invalides is one of the most visited tourist attractions in Paris, and he remains, along with Charlemagne, Joan of Arc, Marshal Conde and others, one of the embodiments of the French military tradition.

| | |
|---|---|
| **1742** | Blücher born. |
| **1745** | "God Save the King" performed for the first time. |
| **1756** | At the beginning of the Seven Years' War, Blücher enlisted in the army of the king of Sweden. |
| **1759** | Captured by the Prussians, Blücher changed sides and became a Prussian hussar. |
| **1760** | George III became king of Great Britain. |
| **1769** | Napoleon, Wellington, and Ney born in the same year. |
| **1770** | Cambronne born. |
| **1774** | Louis XVI became king of France. |
| **1777** | Peregrine Maitland born. |
| **1778** | Napoleon arrived in France and began military school. |
| **1783** | Cavalie Mercer born in England. |

**1789**
The French
Revolution
begins

**1804**
Napoleon crowns himself
and Josephine emperor
and empress

1790

1810

**1812**
Napoleon invades
Russia in June

**1814**
Napoleon
abdicates the
throne and
is given the
island of Elba

Timeline

| | |
|---|---|
| **1789** | French Revolution began. |
| **1792** | "La Marseillaise" sung for the first time. |
| **1793** | King Louis XVI and Marie Antoinette executed. The Revolutionary Wars, between France and most of the other European powers, began. |
| | "Heil dir im Siegerkranz," composed by Heinrich Harries, to the melody of "God Save the King." |
| **1795** | Napoleon dismissed the Paris crowd with "a whiff of grapeshot." |
| **1796** | Napoleon took command of the French army in Northern Italy. |
| | Wellington sailed for India. |
| **1799** | Napoleon carried out a military coup and became first consul. |
| **1804** | Napoleon crowned himself and Josephine emperor and empress. Napoleon raised 18 men to the rank of marshal of the Empire. |

**March 28, 1815**
Britain, Prussia, Austria, and Russia renew the Treaty of Chaumont, which is directed against Napoleon

**October 17, 1815**
Napoleon arrives at St. Helena Island, where he will spend the rest of his life

**February 26, 1815**
Napoleon leaves Elba with 600 members of his Imperial Guard

**July 6, 1815**
The allied armies enter Paris

## 1815          1816

**June 16, 1815**
Battles are fought at Quatre-Bras and Ligny

**June 22, 1815**
Napoleon abdicates the throne

**June 18, 1815**
The Battle of Waterloo rages

| | |
|---|---|
| **1805** | Napoleon and his marshals won their greatest victory at Austerlitz. |
| | Wellington returned from India. |
| | The British Navy won its greatest victory at Trafalgar. |
| **1807** | Napoleon placed his older brother on the throne of Spain. |
| **1808** | The Duke of Wellington landed with British troops in Portugal. |
| **1812** | |
| **May** | British Prime Minister Spencer Perceval assassinated. |
| **June** | The United States declared war on Great Britain. |
| | Napoleon invaded Russia. |
| **September** | Napoleon entered Moscow. |
| **October** | Napoleon retreated from Moscow. |
| **1813** | Napoleon fought on the defensive, lost the Battle of Leipzig. |
| **1814** | Napoleon abdicated the throne, was given the island of Elba. |
| | The Congress of Vienna convened to redraw the map of Europe. |
| | Peace between the United States and Great Britain is signed on Christmas Eve. |
| | Blücher is made a Prussian field marshal and a Prussian prince. |
| **1815** | |
| **January 8** | Andrew Jackson defeated British at Battle of New Orleans. |
| **February 26** | Napoleon left Elba with about 600 members of his Imperial Guard. |
| **March 1** | Napoleon landed at the Golfe de Juan, very close to Cannes. |
| | He issued a Proclamation to the French people. |
| **March 7** | News of Napoleon's escape reached the czar, the Austrian emperor, and the Prussian king in Vienna. |
| **March 11** | The British people received the news of Napoleon's escape in *The London Times*. |
| **March 20** | King Louis XVIII fled Paris in the morning. Napoleon entered Paris that evening, to a tumultuous welcome. |
| **March 28** | Britain, Prussia, Austria, and Russia renewed the Treaty of Chaumont, directed against Napoleon. |
| **April 17** | Napoleon made Emmanuel Grouchy the 26th marshal of the Empire. |
| **June 1** | Marshal Alexander Berthier, who had been Napoleon's chief of staff for nearly 15 years, fell to his death in the German town of Bamberg. |
| **June 15** | The French Armee du Nord crossed the Sambre River and engaged Prussian troops. |

**June 16**    Battles fought at Quatre-Bras and Ligny, about five miles apart. The French defeated the Prussians at Ligny; the Battle of Quatre-Bras was a draw between Ney and Wellington.

**June 17**    The Prussians withdrew to Wavre. The Anglo-Dutch army withdrew to Mont St. Jean.

**June 18**    Battle of Waterloo raged from 11 in the morning till nine in the evening. By its end, the French are routed, and their remnants are pursued by Prussian cavalry.

**June 19**    Learning of the Battle of Waterloo, Marshal Grouchy extricated his 33,000 men from the area.

**June 20**    Napoleon was back in Paris.

**June 22**    Napoleon abdicated the throne. He retired to Malmaison.

**June 29**    Napoleon left Malmaison, just ahead of Prussians in pursuit.

**July 3**    A convention was agreed to between Marshal Davout, the Parisian commander, and the allied armies.

**July 6**    The allied armies entered Paris.

**July 7**    King Louis XVIII returned to Paris.

**July 15**    Napoleon boarded *H.M.S. Bellerophon* as a captive.

**October 17**    Napoleon arrived at St. Helena Island, where he spent the remainder of his life.

**December 9**    Marshal Michel Ney executed in Paris.

**1820**    King George III died in London. He was succeeded by his son, King George IV.

**1821**    Napoleon died on the island of St. Helena.

**1824**    King Louis XVIII died in Paris. He was succeeded by his younger brother, King Charles X.

**1830**    King Charles X overthrown in a three-day revolution carried out in Paris. He was succeeded by one of his cousins, who became King Louis-Philippe.

**1838**    Victoria became queen of England. Several French leaders were present at the ceremony: among them Marshal Soult.

**1840**    Napoleon's remains were brought from St. Helena to France.

They were interred at Les Invalides in Paris.

**1842**    General Cambronne of the Imperial Guard died at Nantes, France. A bronze statue was erected to him in 1848.

**1847**    Marshal Soult, who had been the chief of staff at the Battle of Waterloo was made a marshal general of France. In her long military history, France has had only four with this title.

**1848**    King Louis-Philippe, who had reigned since 1830, was overthrown in a swift revolution.

The Second French Republic was declared.

Louis-Napoleon, a nephew of Napoleon I, was elected president of the Second French Republic.

**1851**    Louis-Napoleon conducted a military coup that made him emperor of the new Second French Empire.

Marshal Soult died.

Charles Joseph Bonaparte born in Baltimore, Maryland.

**1852**    Marshal Marmont, oldest and last of the imperial marshals, died.

The Duke of Wellington died in London.

**1854**    Peregrine Maitland, of the Grenadier Guards, died in London.

**1862**    Victor Hugo publishes *Les Miserables*.

**1868**    Captain Mercer died near Exeter, England.

Brett-James, Antony, editor, *The Hundred Days: Napoleon's Last Campaign from Eyewitness Accounts* (St. Martin's Press, 1964).

Lord Chalfont, editor, *Waterloo: Battle of the Three Armies* (Alfred A. Knopf, 1980).

Connelly, Owen, et al., *Historical Dictionary of Napoleonic France, 1799-1815* (Greenwood Press, 1985).

Grand Dictionnaire Universel Du XIX Siecle.

Henderson, Ernest F., *Blücher and the Uprising of Prussia Against Napoleon 1806-1815* (G.P. Putnam's Sons, 1911).

Hugo, Victor, *Les Miserables* (first published in 1862).

MacDonell, A.G., *Napoleon and His Marshals* (The Macmillan Company, 1934).

Mercer, General Cavalie, *Journal of the Waterloo Campaign, Kept Throughout the Campaign of 1815* (London, 1927).

*The London Times*: Various dates throughout the year 1815.

Saunders, Edith, The Hundred Days (Longmans, 1964).

Siborne, Captain W., *History of the War in France and Belgium in 1815* (1848).

Stirling, Monica, *Madame Letizia: A Portrait of Napoleon's Mother* (Harper & Brothers, 1961).

Thornton, Michael John, *Napoleon After Waterloo: England and the St. Helena Decision* (1968).

Treitschke, Heinrich von, *History of Germany in the 19th Century*. Translated from the German by Eden and Cedar Paul (London, 1916).

page:

2:    Historical Picture Archive/Corbis
6:    Archivo Iconografico, SA/Corbis
9:    Hulton Archive by Getty Images
13:   Hulton Archive by Getty Images
16:   Victoria and Albert Museum,
      London/Art Resource, NY
22:   Hulton Archive by Getty Images
24:   Hulton Archive by Getty Images
28:   Erich Lessing/Art Resource NY
32:   Hulton Archive by Getty Images
35:   Hulton Archive by Getty Images
36:   Giraudon/Art Resource, NY
41:   Giraudon/Art Resource, NY
48:   Christie's Images/Corbis

52:   Archivo Iconografico, SA/Corbis
56:   General Research, The New York
      Public Library; Astor, Lenox, and
      Tilden Foundation
58:   Hulton Archive by Getty Images
64:   Hulton Archive by Getty Images
68:   Reunion des Musees Nationaux/
      Art Resource, NY
72:   Historical Picture Archive/Corbis
75:   Bettmann/Corbis
86:   Hulton Archive by Getty Images
90:   Bettmann/Corbis
94:   Robert Holmes/Corbis
99:   Hulton Archive by Getty Images

*Cover:* Gianni Dagli Orti/Corbis

**SAMUEL WILLARD CROMPTON** is a historian and biographer with a long list of publications to his credit. He is the author or editor of nearly 20 books, with titles that range from *100 Battles that Shaped World History* to *Pillar to Post: Odysseys in Revolutionary America*. Mr. Crompton teaches both Western Civilization and American History at Holyoke Community College. He has long held an interest in French military history, and earned a certificate in historic conservation and presentation from the Historic Fortress of Louisbourg on Cape Breton, Nova Scotia. He has twice served as a Writing Fellow for Oxford University Press in its production of the 24-volume *American National Biography*.